MW00357046

And I Loved Them...

Voices of a Prison Ministry

By Sister Josephine Migliore, M.S.C.

With
David T. Whitaker

Bonus Books, Inc.

Library of Congress Catalog Card Number: 99-23250

International Standard Book Number: 1-566625-116-8

Bonus Books, Inc.
160 East Illinois Street
Chicago, IL 60611
www.bonus-books.com

Cover art: "The Return of the Prodigal Son," Sister Regina Petersen, M.S.C.

Cover design: Gus Antenorcruz

Printed in the United States of America

And I Loved Them...

This book is dedicated to my own dear mother, a powerful inspiration and teacher from whom I learned that virtue and goodness is "caught," not taught. She was the epitome of selflessness, a trait I detected from my youth and wanted to catch from her. It is also dedicated to each of the hundreds of inmates I met at Cook County Correctional Center, for all they have taught me about faith, trust and love. I cherish the time we spent together — the time we shared, laughed and cried together. These inmates have made my ministry possible through their enthusiasm, openness and encouragement.

I wish to spend
My heaven in doing
good upon the Earth...

One of the many card creations Sister Josephine has received from inmates over the years.

Contents

Introduction

All the good I try to do in this world is inspired by God. That is where I draw the strength and grace to pursue my mission of ministering to incarcerated men. Convincing the recipients of this love that God is its true source is not always easy. They usually thank only me.

Just recently, however, an inmate named William proved an enlightened soul. Although I only ministered to William for a few months, he sent me a note after completing his drug program.

> . . . I really miss being able to talk to you. I felt so close to God when I was with you, almost like if he was in a chair right next to you. I believe that's why I trusted you so much from the first day I met you, to tell you all of my problems and dreams. It was like I was talking to God, because I felt something inside of me, kind of lifting my spirits. I believe that may have been God's presence.

William succinctly articulates what I have been trying to instill in men like him for so long. That's what this book is about. It is about the love of God, and about sharing the love of God. It is about those who are perhaps most in need of our love, those incarcerated for their crimes. It is also about the effects of neglected love by parents, peers, siblings and others. And, it is about the dangerous consequences of substituting addictions for God's love.

My motive for writing this book is not just to share with you my experiences of working with the men of Chicago's Cook County Correctional Center, but to demonstrate the impact volunteers can have on the lives of these inmates, to show how love rather than pity can help them better see and understand God's love for them.

This book also features the true voices of this ministry, introducing you to the men behind the prison numbers. In telling their own stories and sharing their struggles, my hope is that each inmate becomes a person rather than a statistic, a man rather than a criminal.

Throughout this book you will get the look and feel of life behind bars at Cook County jail. You will also become better acquainted with the complexities of the penal system.

In my experiences, inmates usually respond more positively to love than punishment. In fact, "tough love" is what I relied on in my ministry — but you have to remember to incorporate the "love" as much as the "tough." When men like William acknowledge the love they have for God, and the love God has for them, they also acknowledge — perhaps for the first time — the love they have for themselves.

The Prayer of St. Theresa of Avila tells us that, "Yours are the only hands with which He can do His work....Yours are the only eyes through which His compassion can shine upon a troubled world." We are called to be in service to God here on earth, to reach out to others as He would, to be God's eyes, ears, hands and feet. We are also called to see God in the poor, the ill, the imprisoned and the lonely.

It is God who asks us to use our eyes as His to see them, to use our ears as His to hear them, to use our hands as His to touch them, to use our mouth as His to spread His Word, and to use our feet as His to show them the way.

The title of this book, *And I Loved Them*, was inspired by this notion of service to God. In my prison ministry, I have served and been served through God's grace. I have learned so much from the men of Cook County jail, and I have loved them.

— Sister Josephine Migliore, M.S.C.

Acknowledgments

For the last 15 years, I have served as staff and patient counselor for Columbus Hospital and its sister hospital, St. Frances Cabrini Hospital.

It was in the Columbus office of Daniel O'Brien, Vice President of Foundation Development, that I saw the painting of the Father embracing the prodigal son and thought it would be an appropriate cover for this book. Mr. O' Brien told me it was a Rembrandt and that it was used by the well-known author Henri M.J. Nouwen on the cover of one of his many books. It is called "The Return of the Prodigal Son."

Shortly before his death, Mr. Nouwen gave me permission to use this theme. He wrote:

> The story deals not with the human love of an earthly father, but the divine love and mercy in its power to transform death into life.
>
> Leaving home is a denial of the spiritual reality that I belong to God, that He holds me safe in an eternal embrace and that I am indeed carved in the palms of God's hands. Home is the center of my being, where I can hear a voice that says, "You are my Beloved, on you my favor rests." When I hear that voice I know I am home with God and have nothing to fear.

Sister Regina Petersen of the Missionary Sisters of the Sacred Heart, to whom I am forever grateful, did a wonderful job of creating her own version of the famous painting for this book.

I owe special thanks to the sisters who offered me and my ministry their love and support, and to my family and my institute, which allowed me to volunteer at the jail for the past 15 years.

My thanks as well to the many friends who have encouraged me in my work and contributed generously for books, stamps, rosaries, etc. Also, thanks to the many magazine publishers who offered me free subscriptions to their publications.

My dear sister, Sister Innocent, passed away shortly after this book was completed. I thank her for her prayers, encouragement and understanding in all my years. To M.J. Gapp for her many contributions and her help, and to Julie Mathers and Maryanne for deciphering and typing so many letters and stories. To my sister-in-law Mary, who would appreciate prayers for healing.

To David Whitaker, who prepared for the task of co-writing this book by visiting the jail with me — to get the feel for the ministry, the inmates and the staff — and for his untiring commitment to getting this book completed.

My sincere thanks to Mary Bottalla and to all of those whose financial and moral support helped make this book possible, especially my close friend of many years, Ron Moretti, and my dear friends at the hospital, Dr. Dan Hurley, and Dr. Leonard J. Cerullo and his associates; I am forever grateful for your generosity.

To Saint Frances Xavier Cabrini, the founder of the Missionary Sisters of the Sacred Heart, for setting such a profound example of living life in service to God.

Finally, to the Holy Spirit, who has been my guide for these many years . . . and Mary, the Mother of God, who has always been with me.

Preface

I met Sister Josephine more than two years ago and accompanied her to Cook County jail with the aim of writing a newspaper article on her prison ministry. After discovering the true nature of her work — the depth of her impact, the strength of the relationships she had built and the compelling stories she had collected over the years — I agreed to help her compile her experiences in a book.

Sister's story is one of love and courage, faith and forgiveness, commitment and compassion. But it is also about those who have felt lost, broken, hopeless and worthless. In this book, the inmates Sister has come to know and love candidly express their moments of weakness and despair, their bouts with fear and depression. They acknowledge their sins and recognize their punishment. These men also share their optimism, their innocence and kindness, their sense of humor, their spiritual awakening and their hope of salvation.

In her interactions with these men, Sister challenges each of us to learn from them, to take personal responsibility in our own lives, to discover freedom with discipline and faith with action. I am privileged to have witnessed her work firsthand and to help her share her ministry with you. Above all, I am honored to share her friendship.

— **David T. Whitaker**

Foreword

I never imagined I'd meet someone like Sister Josephine at Cook County Correctional Center. But, like a lot of inmates, I had seen her walking the halls now and then and was curious about what she did at the jail. One afternoon I ventured into a prayer service I had heard about and there she was.

You must know, I had reached a point in my life where religion had no appeal to me. Though I had been flustered by previous exposure to such gatherings, Sister Josephine quickly and quietly put my fear and inhibition to rest. Her spirit and optimism engulfed the room the moment she spoke. She let us know her aim was not to pass judgment, but to nourish our ailing spirits. To have the patience to encourage men like me, men with seemingly hopeless circumstances, takes a special kind of person.

Many of those Sister comes in contact with are on the verge of mental and spiritual breakdown. They are facing frightening legal consequences. Many have given up on themselves and their future.

The environment doesn't help. Like the building's cold character, its inmates are often lifeless. There is a very real sense of mistrust and disappointment among them. Commitments and promises are viewed as pacts meant to be broken. Despite the misery, Sister Josephine keeps coming, keeps exposing the bright side of life to those willing to listen.

Through her many contacts with inmates and their families, Sister Josephine not only nourishes these ills, but challenges them. Procrastination is ignored, promises and commitments are not. The human spirit is alive no matter the circumstances. She leads by example.

With so many people on the outside convinced her efforts are futile, Sister Josephine carries on, strengthened by such lazy skepticism. Restoring the human spirit is her purpose. The delicacy and compassion with which she pursues her mission is like nothing I've ever known.

Sister Josephine is also endowed with an unbiased concern of religious preference. With her, there is no attempt at traditional "conversion," rather a genuine tolerance for individual choice. Sister Josephine seems instinctively aware of the dangers of projecting personal beliefs on people, knowing such a disposition may well be the tenet which severs the lines of communication. At the same time, her every movement, her attitude and approach to life, is a spiritual act. There is no hidden agenda.

A common misnomer with and among inmates, especially those who have been subjected to the ruins of alcoholism and substance abuse, is that those who haven't "been there" are unable to understand the difficulties they confront. While to some degree this may be true, I have encountered several people who dispel this myth with their overwhelming sense of empathy and sheer eagerness to learn.

Sister may never know the futility nor the insanity that captivates the lives of those she touches, but by being on the front lines she has witnessed the effects of a soul devoid of human spirit. She may not have resuscitated everyone she has come in contact with, but she has never stopped trying, never stopped listening, and never stopped loving.

Today there is a resounding cry to do something about the crime, violence and drugs besieging society. Politicians build platforms promising restoration, but their words echo off hallowed halls. Sister Josephine has traveled those halls, her words backed by her presence and commitment. This book serves as testament to the lives she has touched.

Through her words and those willing to share their stories, you too will walk the halls of incarceration, and discover hope and love in a most unlikely place. To meet and come to know Sister Josephine the way I have is to experience the process of transformation, a transformation of which I, my family and countless others are forever grateful.

May you be motivated by her spirit, as I was, and act upon that inspiration.

— Scott Carlberg
Dixon Penitentiary
Dixon, Illinois

1

Discovering A Ministry

I'll never forget the very first time I walked through the gates of Chicago's Cook County Correctional Center. I was accompanying a fellow sister, Sister Renee Kittleson, on one of her frequent visits to the jail.

After being cleared through several security check points, where our bags were searched each time, we made our way toward one of many buildings made of drab, yellow brick. Upon entering this dormitory, where more than 500 men were being held, upon seeing and feeling the spiritless confines of its walls, upon meeting the blank stares of its inhabitants, I knew I had found my place.

We had driven from St. Francis Cabrini Hospital — where we lived and worked — on the west side to the immense south side complex at 26th Street and California. The dormitory we entered was called Division #8. It houses inmates participating in a substance abuse program on the first floor, but the first inmates we saw were lined up on benches, some in handcuffs, waiting for their turn to see a doctor.

Their faces told part of the story — tired, lost, hopeless, afraid — an array of emotions and circumstances that couldn't be controlled, landing them here. Still, there was life in their eyes, a sense that things could only get better.

"Get these handcuffs off me," came a shout from one inmate just inside a doorway off the corridor. "I don't want to stay here," the 19-year-old inmate continued to yell. I approached the inmate but an officer told me to leave him alone. "I simply want to pray for him," I told the guard. He stubbornly conceded and I began to pray aloud. The inmate began mumbling something and seemed to be calmed by the prayer.

I then turned and talked with the inmates lined up in the hallway. I remember faint smiles and drifting cigarette smoke that caused my eyes to tear. Some offered a "Hello, Sister," others asked for a piece of candy, a cigarette, a rosary. Another guard warned the inmates to keep in line. He also warned me to be careful handing out rosaries that might be used as gang-related symbols.

As I talked with these men briefly, I wondered what kind of impact I could have on the spirit of this place, on officers who seemed to see themselves as both safeguards of society and administers of punishment, and on inmates who viewed themselves as victims, some unwilling to take responsibility and control of their lives, thus making a prison of their own heart and soul. I wondered how long most inmates were held in this jail and how long it would take to build their trust. I also wondered how often I could visit with them.

Fourteen years later, at age 83, Sister Josephine is still at it. It's Thursday morning and, as usual, she's in a hurry. Rummaging through her cramped, windowless office she quickly stuffs religious booklets, prayer cards, a handful of rosaries and what looks like a condensed version of the New Testament into three plastic shopping bags. Once again, she's headed to jail.

Readying her spiritual sales kit for a trip to the lock-up has been part of her weekly routine since that first visit so many years ago. Offering counseling, prayer services, religious materials and friendship to the sojourners of this judicial rest stop is more than a volunteer duty, it's her life mission.

Despite her age, she shows little sign of slowing down. Standing a mere five feet tall and outfitted in the traditional habit of the Missionary Sisters of the Sacred Heart — a gray crew-neck dress, white blouse buttoned at the collar, hair pushed underneath a tra-

ditional, gray veil, and sturdy, black shoes binding her small feet —
Sister Josephine seems the prototype of the sweet, little nun. While
her gentle poise and compassionate instincts dominate, a hearty determination emerges as she encounters the obstacles of her crusade.

Adjusting her large, round glasses and peering thoughtfully
into swollen shopping bags, Sister seems comfortable with what
she's packed for today's trip.

The weather and the Chicago Transit Authority (CTA) often
determine if Sister Josephine will get to the jail by 8 a.m., her self-
imposed start time. If she arrives early, she usually has time to meet
with several men individually before leading her prayer service.

Sister slips a key into her office door and lifts her bags over her
shoulder. As a staff and patient counselor at Columbus Hospital,
which rests among stately three-flats and residential high rises in
the city's Lincoln Park neighborhood, Sister Josephine's job descrip-
tion includes visiting patients, not prisoners. But with more than 60
years of service to the church, she does both.

Sometimes a volunteer or two will accompany Sister to the
jail, but for the last several years it's been difficult to recruit any
help. Some worry about the neighborhood, others the inmates.
Some wonder why she goes at all.

This day she's hampered by sore knees and a lower back weak-
ened by the onset of osteoporosis, but Sister Josephine still marches
purposefully toward the building's menacing black-iron front gate.
A wind-blown rain shower doesn't make her trip any easier.

Two uniformed guards see her coming and step out of a security booth. Though stern-faced, each greets her politely. Sister instinctively hands over her valuables. They examine each bag with
thorough inattention. Sister Josephine rolls her soft, brown eyes and
a smile creeps over her smooth, olive-skinned face. It's all part of the
routine, and each day reminds her of the first.

On that first day I also visited the hospital unit on the second floor of Division #8. An inmate named Victor was lying in

bed ill. "Is there anything I can do to help?" I asked. "I need a drug program," he said. "No one listens to me, but I'll never lick this thing unless I get help."

I went directly to the office of the chief psychiatrist at the time, and told him about Victor's plea. He seemed receptive to the idea. I continued making rounds and returned to Victor's bed later in the day. His broad smile told me our mission was accomplished. "If God works so dramatically without me praying," Victor said, "heaven only knows what would happen if I started to do so."

That day I witnessed the way in which the Lord could touch men like Victor through me, and I realized that Sister Renee brought me to the jail to show me the work that lay ahead. Not long after this encounter, Victor wrote me a letter. It was the first letter I would receive from an inmate. At that time, I could never have imagined how many letters I would receive in the years ahead.

March 9, 1983

Dear Sister,

Hope this letter finds you in good health and spirits. I am currently in my third week of the "Substance Abuse Program" which you were instrumental in obtaining for me. I believe it was a miracle and a blessing, the first I experienced first-hand . . .

Living in a therapeutic community can at times be a test of one's patience and sincerity about just what he values and wants in his life. As I've already made up my mind and heart, the act of submitting is a bit lighter than it would be if I were still in confusion about good and evil, right and wrong, and how they play into my life each day. Sister, I needed this program to help me clarify my deep feelings and the direction for utilizing my efforts for the maximum results.

My goals are not so out of the norm. At 33, I feel a strong sense of wanting more security in my life. I can look back on my younger days and I gasp visualizing how "crazy and carefree" I lived my life. I must also tell you I am sorry for not playing it straight. However, I have a sureness without doubt that the fast, run-around, no-value, caution-to-the-wind life I led was not what it was built to be. It was fruitless and mostly beset with illusions, leaving one drained and empty — both emotionally and spiritually.

I was raised in a Catholic environment — elementary and high school — to which I attribute my solid foundation of what is right and wrong. I thank God that I possess the will and desire to bring my life around to where it should be after my experience with so many negative influences.

. . . My future will depend on my strength and determination as I've burned all my bridges with the people that loved me — or so it seems. I stand to go forward alone! In a way, that gives me an empty and scared feeling. In a way it gives me relief because I've learned the effects of my failures upon others and upon myself. If failure be my fate, I'd choose to go alone.

. . . I would ask for your prayers Sister since I saw you at work once and was left speechless! I'm convinced the Lord brought you to Cermak [prison hospital] as his Personal Representative! I'll never forget that day!! When people ask me how I got to this program in record time, I just grin and say "You wouldn't believe it if I told ya!" And they wouldn't! So I keep you and that day very close to my heart!! Shows that Jesus didn't lose faith in me as I was sure He had ample reason to!!! I will be calling on Him very much in the future . . .

As I'm 100% sure you have a great amount of influence with Our Father, would you please remember my mother, Ann, in your prayers? I worry about her a lot — alone and afflicted with alcoholism — it just isn't fair. My mother was a nurse for 25 years and dedicated her whole life to other people. She raised my sister and me by herself when my dad left our family years ago. And please remember a young lady named Nicole, who I am in love with. Our future looks dim! I don't blame her for thinking I am a risk for a relationship. I ask for strength for her to do what she feels is right regardless if it includes "us" or not! I love her for she is a very good person deserving of happiness and peace of mind. Tell Jesus if He knows I will be a flop to please take Nicole away from me!!!! She really is too good a lady to be hurt that badly! Trust me and my judgment. The Lord could utilize this woman for a great deal of good and usefulness to other people in a positive way . . .

Sister, if I'm released from this bondage you can expect a visit. Perhaps there is something I can do for you. Please don't hesitate to ask and please say hello to Sister Renee for me. I met her last week!! Thank you both for all the efforts you both make in coming to this unhappy place!! There is no sunshine in jail unless it walks in the gates, and it does on the days you come.

For more than a year, Sister Renee and I traveled to the jail together, but from the outset I worked independently of her. I am sure Sister Renee recognized that I almost immediately felt comfortable at the jail because she never made any attempt to direct my activities. I believe she felt it best that I discover the promise of this ministry on my own time and in my own way.

Still, it was through her introduction that I discovered the gift of helping men like Victor help themselves. When Sister Renee was transferred to Seattle, where she currently serves as a prison chaplain, I think she was secure in the knowledge that I would continue the work she began. She has been my inspiration and my friend ever since.

"Hello, Sister. How are ya!" smiles a plump guard manning a long, white desk at a security checkpoint on the building's first floor.

Two other officers leaning against a counter top that surrounds the desk offer her a respectful nod. Flipping her grocery bags on to the counter, Sister Josephine offers each a warm greeting before more firmly declaring, "We're having a service at 1:30 p.m. Please remember to announce it." She turns to her volunteer and whispers, "You have to be assertive in this place."

Sister Josephine realizes security is the primary function of jail, that the job of the officers is to maintain order, and that at times her mission may clash with theirs. Although some officers may look wary on her, gaining their respect and trust is as important to her work as reaching the spirits of the inmates. It's not always easy. An officer once accused her of offering a religious medal as a gift to an inmate who later tried to commit suicide by swallowing it. Sister Josephine scoffs at the charge, insisting she's never brought a medal into the jail.

The 12-step substance abuse program housed in Division #8 is run by the Gateway Foundation. All 350 male inmates of the program suffer alcohol or drug addictions and have been ordered or granted admission to the program while awaiting trial, sentencing or serving county time (less than a year).

The building's pale beige walls, white-tiled floor and sterilized scent emit an aura much like that of a hospital, but the roaming eyes of well-armed guards, the rattling slam of thick metal doors and the weary faces of inmates serve as clear reminders of the distinctions. While depression, fear and suspicion control the climate in Division #8, it is considered a minimum security area. Sister Josephine points out that this is nothing like general population.

Though she has often received permission to visit inmates all over the complex, Sister was assigned to Division #8 and her jurisdiction is usually limited to this structure. Within these confines, she's built a ministry that reaches out to those who have wounded and been wounded in life, a ministry that aims to demonstrate the power of spiritual faith, and how the practice of such faith can impact, and alter, one's life.

It didn't take long to realize that everything I had done and everywhere I had been had prepared me for this mission. God had been sowing the seed for this ministry from my youth.

Raised in a small town in New Jersey, I can remember teaching my companions about God when I was just eight years old. My group of friends used to sneak around the ushers and attend the adults-only Parish Mission Services.

As a high school student, I day-dreamed of telling everyone about God. This phase eventually led me to ask my mother for permission to enter the Dominican Novitiate, to study to become a nun. Her response was firm. "You are not even capable of walking straight, and you already want to take on such an important life decision?"

I struggled through three years of teacher's training school instead, and was eventually permitted to join the Missionary Sisters of the Sacred Heart of Jesus, as my sister had a year earlier.

I taught English to elementary school children in Brooklyn, NY, for 10 years. Taking college courses on weekends and in the summer, I began studies for a Masters degree in English Literature. I came to Chicago the first time to attend Nurses Training School. Despite my nightmares of giving injections, I completed my courses and became supervisor of a floor at Columbus Hospital. I also taught in the School of Nursing and received my Masters in Nursing Education and Counseling.

After six years of nursing I was sent to Seattle to become Director of Nursing and Nursing Services. With 90 mischievous student nurses, I had my hands full. This is where I learned the art of "tough love." After more than 35 years, some of these students continue to correspond with me.

When I was named Administrator of Child Care at a home for neglected children in West Park, NY, I was given one day's notice. Leaving Seattle was difficult, but this was part of the job. For three years I worked with abandoned children before being elected as an Assistant to the Superior General. With this post, I moved to Rome and spent close to nine years making visits to our missions around the world.

In 1983, at the age of 70, I returned to Chicago as a Pastoral Advocate to patients at St. Francis Cabrini Hospital, where I met Sister Renee, and later moved to Columbus Hospital in 1990.

My adventures and relationships with people of all ages and all cultures taught me to better understand the poor, the disenfranchised, the homeless and the imprisoned. All of these experiences, I am now convinced, were God's way of preparing me for the ministry of working with inmates.

"Where is David?" Sister Josephine asks a guard whom she seems most friendly with. "Check the library upstairs," he tells her.

David, 26, is awaiting sentencing after being convicted on stalking charges. Throughout his 21-month incarceration at Cook County jail, he has prayed with Sister Josephine, shared jokes, talked of his family upbringing and discussed his case in great detail with her. He has always denied any guilt in the charges brought upon him. Sister Josephine believes him. But to her, it doesn't matter.

As difficult as it may seem to forgive, especially for victims or the families of victims who have suffered at the hands of criminals, Sister Josephine sees it as a duty of Christianity, if not humanity. "It's the true test of faith," she explains to her volunteer. "If you cannot forgive," she says simply, "then you should never say the Our Father."

I don't ask the inmates to reveal the reason for their incarceration, but they usually tell me. The degree of their crime is not important to me, only that they realize true healing involves a process of acceptance. I am here to listen, not judge, to show these men that someone cares, whether they are guilty or not.

Many people ask me, "What about the victims?" Well, I care very much about the victims and their families, but I also care about people who have gone to jail for committing crimes. They in many ways are the weakest, the most needy among us. They are in great need of discipline, but also of some self-worth that enables them to understand what has brought them here and that will help prepare them to either return to society or endure their time in prison.

In accepting the unconditional love of God, they are better able to accept their personal responsibility as well as their punishment. When they discover love of God, they discover love of self and others. Then, they can begin to understand forgiveness.

Those who are guilty still must live with what they have done for the rest of their lives, but we cannot simply dismiss their existence. We all have to practice what Jesus practiced: forgiveness. If we truly believe our faith, then we have no other choice but to forgive.

Sitting at a table in the building's makeshift library, David looks up from a book he's reading and beams at the sight of Sister Josephine standing in the doorway. He scurries over to her and hugs her around the shoulders. "I tried calling you," he says in his thick, New York accent. "Some sister told me she didn't think you were coming. I'm glad you're here."

Like the rest of the inmates at Cook County, David is dressed in a khaki union suit with black lettering imprinted across the back that reads D.O.C. (Department of Corrections). The white Nike running shoes he wears were sent from home.

With the permission of a guard, David pulls a few chairs into the hallway to talk privately. As he sits, David anxiously launches into the latest on his case. He says he's happy with the selection of the judge who will oversee his sentencing and is confident the judge will consider his time served and order probation.

Sister Josephine sits patiently as David talks about the wavering support of his family and the frustrations of his incarceration. As a fellow inmate pushing a mop eases closer to the one-way conversation, David pauses momentarily and whispers, "You gotta be careful what you say. You can get labeled in here."

"Oh, you can't worry about them," Sister Josephine tells him. "Concentrate on yourself." David surrenders a smile and responds, "I have to worry about them, Sister."

Having been raised Catholic, David strayed from the church as a teenager. He also discovered an escape in alcohol. "When I got here," he tells Sister's volunteer, "I was spiritually bankrupt."

When he arrived at Cook County jail, David was also amazed to see a nun. "She runs around here like a 40-year-old," he says of Sister Josephine. "At first, I was apprehensive about talking to her." When he did, he says, "She didn't preach to me. I developed a friendship with her, a trust. Now I can talk to her about anything."

It took some time before David would talk with me. He quizzed other inmates on who I was and how I could be of help. One day he asked to speak with me but later came up with an excuse not to. I expressed that when he was ready I would be happy to see him.

When he finally was ready, it was on a day that, for security reasons, I was unable to call the men out of the dorm. An inmate had escaped a week earlier and the officers were very strict about inmate movement. Instead I was given permission to talk to them inside. I entered a room full of smoke with a radio blasting and no privacy. Then I moved closer to a corridor leading to their cells. "You can't go there. Sorry, but you are prohibited," a guard told me, so I took two chairs to a corner of the day room. Because of the thickness of the smoke in this window-less room, an inmate brought me a cup of water to ease my coughing.

After talking with two other inmates, David approached me and introduced himself once again. He was very polite and perhaps a bit nervous. We kept the conversation on the trivial side, but it was a start.

From then on, David always wanted to talk with me first. I learned that, like me, he was an Easterner. His wife had divorced him and he left New York to pursue higher learning and a new life in Chicago.

David often seemed more concerned with his children than his own predicament. He worried about how far away he was and the fact that he had little access to his children by phone. "She [his ex-wife] is telling lies, as usual, when I call. She speaks to the children against me and refuses to take them to church in preparation for the Sacraments," he would tell me.

Because his wife was now living with another man, David's frustration mounted. But his ex-wife had little to do with why he was in jail.

> As you enjoy your continued liberty, I'll be struggling to make the best out of my continued incarceration. Last week I was found GUILTY on one count of stalking . . .
>
> Sr. Josephine, I must let God continue to carry me. One of the best things you taught me is that God is a just God. When I was found guilty I still recalled, "God is a just God." It's not easy being 100% innocent and on my way to the penitentiary! However, I must also remember that all things happen in God's time and not mine. I have "faith" that God's justice will shine during my appeal by eventually clearing my name from all these false charges. He's carried me thus far and "footsteps" will continue to carry me. For now, as I am facing probation or four to ten years away from my children, I *must* keep the faith or at least fake it 'til I make it. . . . I'll put it in God's hands; I know He hasn't or won't abandon me.

David had taken a young woman out on a date in Chicago. According to David, the evening didn't go too well and he decided not to make a friendship of it, which angered the woman. David claims she later accused him of stalking her.

> Sister Josephine, what is my key to get out of this? Is it faith? I don't mean to sound cynical but faith seems to have gotten me into this thing and faith seems to let this perpetuate. Don't get me wrong because I do feel very good about myself (on the inside). I also continue to pray like I have been praying for the last 4 1/2 years, on my knees in the

morning and at night before sleep. I also work on a conscious contact with God and when I am wrong about things I promptly admit it (Step 11 of the 12-Step process). But what scares me is that I really don't think I know how to pray. Worse, I feel that I pray because *I'm afraid not to pray!* That if I don't pray something really bad is gonna happen to me. Although I say I believe in a Loving, Trusting God (New Testament), I am beginning to truly feel that I believe in the God I was taught as a child both in Catholic school and in my home — a punishing God (Old Testament), and Sr. Josephine, I don't feel, or at least I don't "think" I feel, that God is punishing me — and my friends and family — but there is no doubt that I am being maliciously punished.

Whenever David and I talked, the conversation always seemed to come back to religion, and his relationship with God. David's quite a thinker, and he's not been afraid to think out loud to me about his struggle with faith. Many of his letters, I think, served as an outlet for his ongoing dialogue with God.

When I start to "analyze" the situation, things don't sum up. If God is all powerful and all loving, then why do bad things happen to good people? I read the Book of Job and, please excuse me, but so what? Sr. Josephine, it seems too much of a crutch to give God all the credit for anything good in our lives and when circumstances turn sour, just say "Oh, well, some things are out of God's control."

Sr. Josephine, I don't mean to question my faith so much but I need to. If I haven't had a spiritual advisor in my life such as you, I would only further frustrate my faith with these thoughts. I appreciate your being here for me so that I can ventilate my feelings no matter how absurd they may seem . . .

Just weeks later I received another letter from David. This time he seemed to be feeling more comfortable with his faith. "In my soul," he wrote, "I am finding out that decades ago I walked away from the greatest relationship — with God. Sister Josephine, I am 'joyful.' I no longer walk away!"

While she can tolerate the separation of church and state, Sister Josephine does not believe in impeding religious freedom. In the jail, she will talk to whomever wants to talk to her. She believes it is the right of each inmate to continue practicing his or her religion and be afforded religious services, and it is her responsibility to make sure both inmates and officers are reminded of that.

Sister Josephine's first priority, however, is to ease the fear and frustration of incarceration, to lend a friendly ear and a compassionate voice. "They have so much on their mind," Sister tells her volunteer, "that I rarely do anything but listen. We talk and pray."

Since that first day 14 years ago, Sister Josephine has counseled hundreds of inmates, some who have been released back into society and others who have gone on to serve time in penitentiaries. She strives to forge long-term relationships and many inmates have kept in touch with her by mail, including a few on death row. Any time left between her duties at the hospital and her weekly visits to the jail is dedicated to answering 15 to 18 letters a week. One inmate, who had been diagnosed with cancer, sent Sister a letter that included his last Will and Testament. Part of his note read, "When you are contacted about my death either by violence in population or by the cancer, please make sure my things are given to these people. Thanks."

On top of her weekly visits to the jail and ongoing pen pal relationship with dozens of prisoners across the country, Sister has contacted family members and attorneys of certain inmates, written to judges on behalf of inmates facing sentencing and parole hearings and attempted to find employment and housing for many of those released from the system.

David says that what he most looks forward to when Sister Josephine visits is the chance to talk to someone without feeling judged. "This is a very, very lonely place," he says. "If it weren't for a weekly dose of Sister Josephine, I don't know what kind of shape I'd be in right now."

2

Locked in Addiction

As she heads down a long hallway toward a security desk, Sister Josephine wonders aloud why guards have yet to announce her afternoon prayer service over the public address system. Her focus is interrupted by the sound of an inmate rapping his palm against a thick wall of glass that separates him from her. She turns and, upon recognizing the man's boyish grin, smiles and returns his wave.

After motioning a guard at the end of the hallway to electronically unlock a bulky metal door, Sister pulls the heavy door open and slides inside what is referred to by the inmates as "A-House."

"A-House" consists of two large, windowless rooms where inmates of the Gateway substance abuse program meet in groups to discuss the battle with their addictions and listen to guest speakers who claim to have conquered their own dependencies.

Joe embraces Sister Josephine as other inmates remain busy talking in small groups, playing cards and watching television. Taking a seat across from Joe at a large, metal table, Sister Josephine begins quizzing Joe on his emotional health. A few inmates position themselves for their chance to talk with Sister and others look on curiously.

The conversation is interrupted before it begins by an inmate with obvious authority. From his post behind a large wooden desk, he stands before the room and forcefully announces, "A-House! We have guests in the room. Respect our guests. Keep noise at a low level." "A-House, yes sir," respond his fellow inmates in unison before going back to their business.

Sister Josephine listens intently as Joe recounts his renewed strength in avoiding jail house trouble. "Today, Joe chose to prevent conflict rather than pass judgment," he says, referring to himself in the third person. Sister Josephine tells him it is better to avoid trouble. "You can't afford it," she says gently. "It is important for you to be in this program, to concentrate on being a whole man."

At 36, this is Joe's second time through Cook County. While he prefers not to reveal the charges that have brought him here either time, Joe hints they stem from drug abuse and the gang mentality with which he says he was raised. The symbols tattooed down his left arm corroborate his claim to gang ties.

"It has been hard for me to break away from drugs and gangs," he admits, "even in here. After my first arrest [three years ago], I was in GP (general population), where you have to be hooked up with a gang. So I continued to start fights and make trouble," he explains softly. "I even smuggled drugs through the visitation room, but didn't get caught."

Joe certainly isn't alone in tying his incarceration to a history of drug use. According to a 1997 study conducted by The National Center on Addiction and Substance Abuse, the crimes committed by 80% of the adults in U.S. prisons were in some way related to their drug and alcohol abuse.

Because I serve inmates in Division #8, almost all of the men I work with are members of the Gateway substance abuse program. Many have taken the initiative to request being placed into this drug rehabilitation program while others are required to complete it. Their struggle with drugs, as the Gateway program stresses, is a battle that will last a lifetime.

The destruction caused by drugs and alcohol is obvious in a place like this. Some inmates have written to me and put it quite simply, "I am serving a 24-year sentence in the penitentiary, with eight years to complete," wrote one man. "My lust for drugs and money not only cost me my freedom, it has divided my family . . ."

Another wrote, " . . . I began drinking at the age of nine. Alcohol was always around the house. . . . That was when my life started going down hill. I started stealing from stores and back porches. Gradually that led to houses and garages."

Others have delved deeper in describing, and analyzing, their attraction to drugs and alcohol.

> . . . Only 18 years old when fate came into my soul and I decided to drink with the big boys. It's like yesterday remembering my encounter in that lounge. It was like a magnet pulling me in, almost as if it had been waiting for me. The drink itself had my name on it, waiting ever so patiently for me to walk into that lounge and give myself to it unconditionally. Brandy with sweet vermouth topped with a cherry was brought to my lips. Right there in that instant was when everything went dark for me. It was at that moment that the change took place. It was thrilling and exciting all at the same time. The music in the background pounding in my heart as the smoke slowly dropped from the ceiling. Sharply dressed women flirting and smiling as they walked by almost like it was planned for my personal entertainment. The lights, the music, it was all overwhelming to me. This is what I had been missing? . . . It was magic, I thought.

The words of another inmate echo the same type of innocent attraction — drug and drink as loyal friend, a boost to self-esteem and a great escape.

> . . . At the age of 26, my brother introduced me to my first drug, marijuana. It really seemed like it made me happy for the first time in a long time.
>
> I began using cocaine at the age of 30. I was making good money on my job and hanging around with people

who were also using the drug. My first arrest came at the age of 31. I was charged with possession of a controlled substance and given two years probation. While I was on probation I was arrested again for the same thing and sent to prison for three years . . . . While out on home monitor, I went back to the old neighborhood and got caught stealing money for drugs. The judge was not happy to see me and gave me six years in prison. But that was not the worst thing for my brother committed suicide at the age of 38. He was an alcoholic. While I sat in Cook County jail, I began to pray for the first time in years. Wanting to change my life, I decided to go to church one day and that's when I met you . . .

As we all have heard, drugs can be obtained fairly easily in jail and prison. Many times it's brought in by visitors, but there have also been cases where prison personnel were discovered to be the traffickers. Drugs have always been an obstacle to my ministry. Many times I have traveled down to the jail and had to turn around and go back because the inmates were on lock-down so guards could conduct a drug search.

As Sister Josephine and Joe continue to talk about his quest to rid his life of drugs, the room becomes noisy with chatter. Again an inmate stands and declares, "A-House! We have guests in the room. Respect our guests. Keep conversation at a low level." "A-House, yes sir," respond the men.

Getting into the Gateway program upon his latest arrest and meeting with Sister Josephine, Joe says, has helped him discover another side of himself. In "A-House," he tells Sister, he doesn't have to worry about any gang affiliation because it's like its own community within the jail.

An upcoming sentencing hearing will determine if Joe will stay in the program or be released on probation. But, he says he's not ready to be released. "I can feel God's work in my life," Joe says with emotion. "I read the Bible for the first time and now I can't stop reading it. With a few other guys, I started a Bible study group in here. I just hope I get sentenced to this program and can continue to heal myself."

Joe acknowledges to Sister the void he's felt throughout his life. He admits drugs and gangs played a large role in his search to fill that void. "It's taken me a long time to realize it," Joe says, "but I used drugs as a crutch against the pain. But now, Sister, I am a much stronger person since discovering myself through God."

Sister Josephine says she realizes how difficult it must be for someone like Joe to turn his back on drugs when they have been such a constant in his life. So she listens. She listens to what drugs have done to their lives, to their families and to their friends. It is the inmates, she says, who suggest they have put their faith in drugs rather than in God.

Addictions, I believe, are a failure to love God, others and ourselves. At the heart of every sin is a failure to love. We can look into our hearts and see where we have disregarded God's greatest commandments, to love him and one another.

Not only have we sinned, but we have also been sinned against. Other people, even those closest to us, have deprived us of love at different times in our lives. This has left us wounded and scarred. Our addictions make us cling to what others proclaim is the key to the self-fulfillment we lack. The accumulation of wealth and power, the attainment of status and admiration, the lavish consumption of food, drink, drugs or sexual gratification become our spiritual pursuits.

One inmate referred to drinking as a cure all, "a liberation from all my problems of the past. . . . At one time or another," he said, "I had stopped hating beer and started loving it." In a letter to me he went on to write:

> The worst thing was that one was too many for me, but a thousand was never enough. I felt in control for the first time in my life, a new existence had emerged from within, and I liked it.

Childhood dreams, they are our very existence. But, for me, all was given up so quickly. There was no warning, no instruction manual, nothing to say what life would be like having alcohol as my master. The night life, drinking all the time, is a slow painful death without you ever knowing it's killing you.

It was years before I actually found out that it was not I who was in control, but the demons who lived inside my drinks. It was a living, breathing entity lying dormant, devouring everything I was. Every decision that I made was based on if it involved alcohol, or if it cut into my [drinking] time. If a girl didn't drink I had nothing to do with her. The love I would find would be in a crowd of people who worshipped the glass as much as I did.

Another inmate once told me that for many years he truly believed drugs were his god. Another referred to drugs as his lover. Again, what is missing, I believe, is our love of God and self. When we abandon love, denial rules.

I realize for many years, you have tried to extend your hand to help me. However, I was much more calloused in days past and in my distorted thinking I could see your arm extended but what I saw was a closed fist. If I didn't care for myself, then how could anyone else!

This inmate, named Scott, serves as an example that with a disregard for self, alcohol and drugs and other destructive behavior are used as an escape from a world that's become incomprehensible. Recklessness replaces strength and faith in fending off feelings of frustration, confusion and loneliness.

For 16 years now — I'm almost 30 — I have been an abuser of alcohol and cocaine. Sadly, I didn't know then what I readily admit now. I'm an alcoholic and addict! In turn I have spent all these years trying to manipulate my disease and I continued to come up shorthanded. To support my baby I robbed, cheated and lied to anyone who crossed my path. I was in love with my addiction. It always comforted me, so when I felt pain, fear — of myself, and being unwanted — loneliness or despair, I could always count on my lover. Nothing mattered to me except to stay anesthetized; then and only then I felt acceptable to others and the gnawing pain of life and its responsibilities would subside.

After a while the drinking and getting high started losing its flavor. It took more and more to reach my pinnacle. I began acting out in ways I could not understand, waking up in jail cells only to learn of what I had done the night before. The consequences began to matter less and subsequently the jail terms increased.

I can't pinpoint at what age I became addicted, but I do remember the feelings of helplessness and powerlessness every time I attempted to quit or modify — I no longer had the control of my own actions. How many times I promised myself the drink I held in my hand would be the last!

Ironically, Scott's brother was hit and severely injured by a drunk driver years earlier. Scott learned this news when he was locked up in the County jail. Rather than curb his abuse, this incident seemed to compound his problem.

After almost seven years in adult correctional facilities, I was still perplexed by my behavior and recidivism. I could never fathom the thought of alcohol or drugs being the source of my troubles. I had built a wall of denial which could withstand just about anything. I referred earlier to my addiction as "my lover" and I could see no way of enduring without her. No matter where I went, in prison or on the streets, she was with me.

Despite the encouragement of many of his fellow inmates, Scott for a long time resisted attending any of the prayer services I held in Division #8. He finally gave in, but when he came he seldom contributed anything to our group prayers, songs or discussions.

Like many people who suffer from addiction, Scott could not muster the strength — both physically and spiritually — to confront his problem and seek help. He kept waiting for others to recognize it and take responsibility, though he knew deep down that only he could break his dependency and turn his life around.

Until now, you probably only knew the half of it. You see, nobody ever really asked exactly what was going on. Obviously, everyone was aware of my repeated bouts with the law, yet it seemed like all this was not worthy of conversation or was treated as confidential. Nobody said a word or asked any probing questions — maybe for fear of offending me or just because there is no easy way to bring up the subject. Ironically, I was so willing to talk about it. I wanted the family to know exactly what happened and how afraid I was.

You would think going into prison is the most difficult part, but it doesn't compare to the fear that grips me coming out! I remember after my first release in 1987, I was standing in the parking lot looking back at the institution, but instead of an overwhelming sense of joy (which I had expected), I felt empty and alone. Crazy as it may seem, I wanted to go back inside and be with the people who understood me. For God's sake they knew me better than I knew myself. So, naturally it was less than a year that I was back where I thought was the only place I belonged.

Eventually Scott sought out a private meeting with me and opened up a bit about his struggles. His letters, however, always offered more detail, and I think writing about his problems proved to be very healthy for him. He seemed to be sorting through his pain and, at last, searching for some meaning to his life.

By now it may be evident that alcohol and drugs are byproducts of my disease. The real problem is my thinking: How I feel about myself and the world around me. I was born with this disease and I began acting out long before I took my first drink. To my demise, after I took the first one I started a chain reaction and I began suppressing every uncomfortable feeling and emotion. When the meter read full, and I exploded, it was always in negative and destructive ways; hence, my life has been in constant turmoil.

One day Scott was taken from the jail on a bus that delivered him to a court date in the suburbs. It was damp and dreary on his return trip, and as the bus drove through a depressed neighborhood he looked out the window and saw a poor man sleeping on the steps of a church. With rain pouring down on the man and his ragged clothing, Scott thought to himself, "If I don't stop my drinking habits and my lifestyle, I will be just like him. I don't want to be that."

Henri Nouwen has said, "I become a prodigal son every time I search for unconditional love where it cannot be found. God alone can love us unconditionally to the extent of our being left free to leave home. But the Father is always looking for me with outstretched arms to receive me, and whispers again, you are my beloved, and you my son."

Accepting my current situation and the difficulties commonly associated does not relieve me of the suffering. I can say that by not taking flight — especially in substance abuse — it has opened the door to a rich spiritual experience. For enduring my difficulties I am a wiser and more enriched individual. Pain, as much as I would sometimes like, will not die of neglect. God, in His wisdom, knew the paradox in suffering. Through willingness, I am given the strength and avenues to conquer, overcome or accept what may come my way. If not for my sufferings, I may not have been afforded the opportunities, at least to this degree, to grow in wisdom, character, and most importantly, faith.

I don't know that change is the appropriate word to depict what has taken place over the last few years. My preference is to see it as a return to the natural God-created man I was intended to be. As in the case of the prodigal son, I hope it pleases Him well. So, the "change" was when I deviated from this state of being. In the gallows of my mind I have returned home.

Unless we choose to work through our aching emptiness and call out to God for the grace and strength to change, we will very likely fill that void in an unhealthy manner. Loving Father that He is, God promises that He will always supply the grace to help us.

With his newfound faith and wisdom in counseling, Scott helped many of his peers and gained the respect of drug counselors and officers. He was entrusted with the job of clerk and became a voracious reader. Requesting more and more spiritual material, Scott circulated the books and writings among the inmates and staff. All the while Scott seemed to come to grips with the gravity of his crimes, which affected his family greatly and alienated them to the extent that he no longer had contact with any of them. He eventually attempted to reach out for forgiveness by formulating a long letter confessing his misdeeds and expressing his sorrow.

Leaning across the long, metal table in "A-House," Joe tells Sister Josephine that through the Gateway program he's actually met other men who can relate to his goal of one day making his family proud. "That's nothin' I've ever had before," he says.

For many of the inmates Sister has come to know, drugs were just a part of their impoverished surroundings. At an early age, many of these men were exposed to drugs through family members, neighbors or familiar characters of their street. While Sister is aware drug and alcohol abuse tends to be more prevalent in low income areas, she is also quick to point out that it does not discriminate by class or race.

When I first met Mark I wondered how such a handsome, intelligent and pleasant young man could find himself in prison. I was curious, and began to learn more about him.

> Throughout my childhood I was given an enormous amount of love by my parents and family. My childhood was a happy one. My father introduced me to the Boy Scouts where I learned to love the outdoors as he does. My parents took us camping frequently. I got to see every state west of the Mississippi by the time I was 18. I loved camping and traveling.

Mark also learned to play the piano, got fairly good grades in school and was active in school sports. But, he said, drugs became more common in his neighborhood in the late '60s and early '70s.

> I first drank beer in the park like every other kid in the 8th grade. This was a weekend thing at best, never getting out of control. The most serious trouble came from an occasional late curfew. When I was a sophomore in high school, I submitted to peer pressure and smoked my first joint. Within one year I had experimented with almost every drug on the market except heroin and cocaine. They were only yet-to-be's. I still managed to go to school every day, and to fool parents that all was normal.
> ... I tried heroin in 1977. I loved it and it turned out to be my demise. During the first few years my drug dealing subsidized my heroin use, but soon my addiction took over and my dealing days were numbered. I couldn't afford to feed my now $100 a day habit from my profits from dealing drugs. I soon lost all I had accomplished, and I was broke with no income.

Mark was raised to know right from wrong, yet he compromised those values to feed his habit. He was arrested for stealing in 1982 and has been incarcerated five times since. After his third arrest he was told he had contracted the HIV virus.

> I've cheated myself of a wife, a career, even growing old. . . . I try to remain optimistic, but I'm a realist at heart. My days may be numbered, but for now I'm doing fine. I've turned up the flame of my relationship with the Lord. It was never extinguished but got pretty low. Maybe it took all these incarcerations and acquiring a fatal disease to open my eyes. I'm not sorry — better late than never. I am grateful to God for opening my eyes before I pass on.

Mark's parents have always stood by him and were there to greet him upon his latest release. He earned a college degree in prison and is now living with his parents, holding down a job, feeling rather healthy and keeping away from drugs.

Having plumbed the depths of addiction, I think Mark, at age 41, is tired of going back to it. I think he also realizes he cannot succeed in this battle on his own. If he is sincere in staying sober, he will demonstrate it by invoking the intercession of Almighty God, who is all powerful and willing to liberate him. It is up to Mark to show love in action.

"Criminals and prisoners," it has been said, "like all humans, can be destructive, hostile and dangerous individuals. They are prone or capable of doing unloving, evil things. Some of them are thoroughly unlikable people and at times it takes no small effort to see in them any 'spark of the divine.'"

As hard as it may be to find, however, we must remember that very "spark of the divine" lies within each one of us. It may be difficult but we must learn to recognize prisoners as human beings who possess dignity, deserve respect and have human needs and sensitivities like any other person. This is a first step in allowing ourselves to love and forgive them.

Society, parents, friends and the judicial system sometimes seem unmindful of their basic human needs, treating them as things rather than people. I have heard prison guards refer to inmates as animals that need to be locked up in a cage. When some inmates were lining up for confession at one of our services, the same guard said, "What they need is a bullet, not confession." This only reinforces the negative self-image these men have carried all their lives.

Of course, society must be protected from the actions of certain people. But, we mustn't dismiss these people from society. I believe prisoners are loved by God in a special way, a way that sends individuals to them who can demonstrate the care, concern and love of which they are and have been deprived.

Only when exposed to love and concern can those who have been deprived of it begin to understand and accept it. When they decide to love themselves they are more apt to seek out the positive instruments of change.

With so many inmates confined by their dependencies, substance abuse programs such as those run by Alcoholics Anonymous and the Gateway Foundation are an invaluable asset to the prison system. It is important to note, however, that such programs are not available in every institution and are not always offered to the majority of inmates. Still, it is each inmate's challenge to find the courage and self-esteem to pursue a positive path rather than just surrendering themselves to their punishment.

As other men in "A-House" begin to crowd around Sister Josephine, Joe smiles and tells her she is a very popular person. In his many letters to Sister Josephine over the years, Joe has both confided his struggles and expressed his gratitude for her help in guiding him toward God and a new definition of self.

Dear Sister,

I hope this letter finds you in good health. As for myself, I am doing just fine. They came and got me for the program, which I am very happy about. I have to do 90 days inpatient and 90 days out.

. . . As long as I keep my faith in God, the Father Almighty, I neither fear nor worry about anything for my Lord Jesus Christ walks with me today. Since my incarceration, so many things have happened to me for which I cannot account. One of these occurred when I first set my eyes on you, walking through the corridors of Div. #8. I experienced what I cannot explain . . . and I just knew I had to speak with you. When the opportunity presented itself, my heart was filled with joy.

. . . You amaze me managing to visit all of us inmates every week and find time to attend your meetings, and all of the traveling you do. I truly believe it is the work of Our Father which inspires you to continue in God's service . . .

As Joe concedes Sister's time, he leans down to hug her and into her ear says, "When I see you, I'm good 'til Monday, sometimes Tuesday." He then disappears into a cavernous hallway that leads to a row of cells.

3

Searching for Self

Sister Josephine motions an officer to unlock the door to "A-House."
She pulls the heavy door open, steps out into the hallway and into
the path of an inmate and an officer who's guiding him back to his
cell. "Are you here again?" Sister disappointingly confronts the in-
mate. "Hi Sister," he smiles while pushing his stringy dark hair be-
hind his ears. "It's not my fault," the inmate pleads.

Jim suffers from mild mental illness, according to Sister
Josephine, and has been a regular visitor to her prayer services in
the past. The officer tells Sister that Jim has just been examined by
a doctor on the first floor and is being returned to the psychiatric
ward on the third floor, where he is being held. Sister decides she
will join them on the elevator ride so she can pay a visit to the
prison hospital, which is run by Cermak Health Services and lo-
cated on the second floor of Division #8. Jim is anxious to tell Sister
Josephine why he's returned to jail.

"It wasn't my fault," he begins again. Jim goes on to explain to
Sister that he was arrested for stealing three sandwiches from a fire
station refrigerator. "There was no one there, the doors were open
and I needed something to eat. I walked inside and got a sandwich
from the kitchen and then I was caught."

The elevator stops at the second floor and as Sister Josephine
and her volunteer begin to step out, Jim asks Sister if she has any

candy. "Are you coming to the prayer service today?" she asks him. Jim nods his head excitedly and glances at the stone-faced officer. "Then you'll get some after the service," she assures him as the doors begin to close.

Again Sister's bags are searched, this time at a security checkpoint just off the elevator. Across from the security booth are two cramped rooms that serve as nurses' stations. Inside one room, a handful of men and women wearing white lab coats are busy doing paperwork. In the hallway outside, dim-lighting, barred doorways and watchful eyes confirm the duality of this hospital.

An officer posted at the security checkpoint explains that Cermak hospital holds prisoners who are not stable enough to mix with those in general population or in the psychiatric ward upstairs. Many, he says, are in need of medical attention or are under observation. At times, he says, high profile inmates are held here, protected from inmates who might pose a threat to them. Occasionally, the hospital holds inmates placed on suicide watch.

Another officer escorts Sister and her volunteer through two sets of thick-celled doors — one just beyond the security checkpoint and another farther down the hallway. "You do realize where you are," the officer says by way of warning Sister's volunteer to the nature of inmates being held here.

As Sister approaches the second set of doors, an elderly inmate can be seen wandering in the hallway and heard singing a song in a language that Sister recognizes as Polish.

Dressed in a long, white gown and brown slippers, the man's singing gets softer as she approaches. "That's okay," Sister says gently as she walks through the cell doors. The man's singing stops. He acknowledges her by tilting his head and mumbling incoherently. "Yes, that's okay. That's very nice," she tells him with a smile.

The long, dark hallway is lined with small, private cells. Many of the cells this day are empty, but Sister peeks her head in to those that look occupied. In one room a man lies in bed groaning. In another, a man is strapped to his bed at the wrists but seems to be *sleeping peacefully. Her uniformed escort reminds Sister to be very careful in this wing of the jail.*

At the beginning of my ministry in jail, I spent a lot of time visiting inmates held in Cermak hospital. I have seen many men, even very young men, strapped down to their beds. It is not something I like to see, but jail officials insist it is necessary to take such precautions with those who are considered mentally unbalanced. They are believed to be a danger to themselves and others.

At one point I was a regular guest to group meetings between inmates and the jail's psychiatrist. I would only say a few words at these meetings and let the inmates know I was available if any of them wanted to talk with me.

I once met a man with AIDS who was being held in the hospital. He seemed to be dying and his sister begged the authorities to release him so he could die at home. She was unsuccessful.

The man told me he was Catholic so I asked him if he would like us to help him make his peace with God. He was very receptive to the idea. I set up a service and brought a Deacon with me one day. The Deacon gave him Holy Communion and we had him offer an Act of Contrition. The next time I visited the hospital, I was told the man had died. I prayed the Lord took him into heaven.

I have seen many cases of AIDS in the hospital. One man's wife and child contracted it from him. He told me how poorly his wife and child lived, that their apartment was without furniture. Through my work at Columbus Hospital, I was able to arrange to have a bed donated to her. I lost track of this man after our few meetings.

Another inmate whom I regularly met with was so filled with delusion he was convinced that I was an angel. In letters to me he seemed unsure of my human existence. He also wrote, "I have emotional hang-ups and interpersonal conflicts. I'm trying to overcome irrational and illogical behavior, and I want to eliminate my undesirable, self-defeating reactions."

This man said he contemplated suicide to avoid a lengthy prison sentence. During his stay at the jail, I was able to take care of many of his needs. He had a Bible but could not see to read it, so I arranged for him to have an eye test and then paid for his glasses.

I continued corresponding with him for 10 years. He visited me upon his release and then he didn't contact me for a few years. Two years ago I received a letter from him in which he told me he was incarcerated again for Driving Under the Influence of Alcohol. Somehow, he had accumulated some money and wanted to pay me back for all I'd done for him. He sent me a check for $300 and wrote:

> I'm demonstrating my love for you and my gratitude. I'm sending you $300 all together, for a convict that is equivalent to $3,000 dollars. You encouraged me to hope and pray, and I took your advice. Now there is a great possibility for me to return to society and become more productive, and live a more meaningful and rewarding life. Also, I'll be able to contribute something positive to my children. I couldn't have done any of those things had I carried out my first plan [of suicide]. I am trying to discipline myself by reading psychological literature. I read and reread the book you sent to me years ago, called *Help Yourself*, by John N. Lenbo. It is highly enlightening and I appreciate your sending it to me.

This man's troubles illustrate the ongoing inner conflict that many inmates battle. They want and need reform but lack the discipline, courage and self-esteem to do so. I believe this goes hand-in-hand with our human struggle with faith. Again, to love God is to love ourselves and others. The resistance to give ourselves to God and accept His unconditional love can be a powerful force, especially for those who have never been introduced to love, whose low sense of self-worth was established early in life and reinforced time and again.

That's not to say that we are not accountable for our actions. With God's love comes the accountability of practicing our faith — loving ourselves and others. Yet, God's love does not cease when we fail. It is ever-present for us to accept joyfully.

Walking more quickly now, Sister Josephine continues down the dim hallway of Cermak hospital. She eventually reaches a bright and spacious room filled with three wooden tables surrounded by gray, plastic chairs. The cement walls of this surprisingly cheery room are decorated with the colorful work of the hospital's patients and in one corner of the room stands a large, classroom chalkboard.

Around one of the tables sit two women and three men. The women are leading an arts workshop for the inmates. The women smile at Sister Josephine as she enters the room. Sister introduces herself to the inmates as the officer looks on. Sister congratulates the women for the good work they are doing and to each of the inmates, she says, "God bless you."

As Sister turns to leave the room, she seems distressed by those, like Jim, who often lack the emotional capacity to bear responsibility for the actions that have brought them here, or the cognizance to understand their circumstance.

So many of the men suffer from mental illness, even those who aren't considered mentally ill. Many of the inmates are dealing with social and emotional problems long before abusing drugs and alcohol. The lack of a loving and nurturing family early in life is often what destroys their hope, identity and self-esteem. It is this troubled upbringing that tends to steer them toward drug and drink.

Kelly is just one inmate whom I came to know that suffered severely from his childhood. When I first met him I knew he carried painful memories.

I remember walking into the dorm area one day and asking if anyone would like to talk with me. I could see Kelly eyeing me as I talked with others, but he wouldn't budge when he had the chance. "How about you?" I finally said to Kelly. He told me he was fine, that he could take care of himself.

Could I trust her? Would she scold me? I am a man and don't need a woman preacher. These were the thoughts that ran through Kelly's mind that day, at least that's what he confided in me three weeks later, when he finally asked to speak with me. It was then that he was able to disclose the hurting boy whom I could already see was in need of love and acceptance.

Kelly told me he was incarcerated in an attempt to steal from a residence. He turned the knob of a door and when he opened it enough to see an elderly woman inside, he ran away. He was on drugs and, like Jim, had nothing to eat and was accustomed to doing what he had to do to get by. In writing his story, he says, "I have made a mess of my life." It is obvious, however, that this mess is not all his doing.

My earliest memory starts at about age five or six. I don't know if my mother was alive at this time or not. I lived at Fullerton and Kedzie [in Chicago], near a candied apple place. There was a Clark Gas Station nearby that I went into and, I don't know what I was doing, but I stole something there which caused the man to chase me and I ran through a glass window. Another man came out of a taxi and rushed over to me, putting a handkerchief to my cut face. I still have a scar under my left eye where the glass cut me. That man saved my eye.

After my mother's death I moved into her brother, Kevin, and his wife's house. This is when the nightmare began since I was beaten for various reasons [by my uncle]. I went to kindergarten with black eyes and bruises all over my body. I had my first sexual experience with my aunt. My grandmother died of cancer when I was seven or eight and that was when I exposed that monster [his uncle, Kevin] for what he was and I ceased being a punching bag.

After this I went to live with my father's mother, Sara, God bless her soul. My brother Billy joined me, while my sister Clare lived with her daughter in Northlake, Illinois. Life was grand, but I followed my brother and became devious. I stole from one person who showed me love, my grandfather Jack. He was great since we were taken places to do many things but I followed my brother always.

My brother and I moved again, this time with Karen and Steve, my mother's sister and her husband. All I can recall is the day we left and my gramps begging me to stay. I stuck with my brother because we were determined to get that guy — our uncle who used to beat us.

Steve and Karen were both alcoholics and we moved with them to Southern Illinois. Nothing bad happened with them except they got tired of their new toys — us — and we were returned. We were placed with a cousin who was too young and had children of her own, so we went back to Karen and Steve. Eventually they found a solution, split us up.

Kelly moved from relative to relative over the next few years and was eventually taken by the Department of Children and Family Services (D.C.F.S) and placed in foster care. He lived with two different families where he continued his drug use. He eventually wound up with another relative, but drugs became the only companion in his early life.

As my disease continued, so did the cost and consequently someone had to pay. It was nothing personal. I never stole from people I knew but either the opportunity presented itself or I looked for the opportunity. I eventually got caught, and was let go time and again.

After a long period, I was accepted at a group home in Princeton, Illinois, called the Covenant House. It was a fabulous place except I still had the desire to medicate my feelings since I did not know how to deal with the pain of life, with what I caused or accepted.

Therefore, I went back to being controlled, once again giving up my will to insanity. I was caught again and ironically I was let go on an I-bond because of an incident that happened here at the C.C.D.O.C. (Cook County Department of Corrections). Well I never went to court so I was picked up and sentenced to the penitentiary at 17 years of age for five years.

. . . When I was released from prison, I still had the same habit plus I was broke. So once again I was off and right away I was back in jail. This time I was 20 and was given six years. I kept up the habit during incarceration, just mildly though, until I got out and was able to promote it wholeheartedly — controlled. I met a very fine girl, so I thought she was my answer but I had to repeat the question again with her. I wanted so much to quit. I knew we could have made it, but no, I had to prove that I could provide what I thought we wanted — to be controlled??

I've surely made a mess of my life thus far. Anyway, in the midst of the addiction, I did the stupid thing again and the consequences are the same. I pleaded guilty on all my offenses to save time; isn't that insane? Anyway, I did my time the same way with similar results except I swore I would never commit a crime again since I wasn't inclined toward that path.

However, my addiction left me with all my prior emotions still lingering on. What was I to do? I went back to the addiction, but not the crime. I worked for my drugs but I was dead inside because I had no peace.

Kelly suffered a stroke shortly after learning additional years had been added to his latest sentence. He often told me I was his only friend in this hostile jail, but then he volunteered to work on the grounds and his supervising officer was very appreciative and kind to Kelly. This was gratifying to me because he worked under her supervision five days a week. I was introduced to her and expressed my thanks for all she had done for Kelly. I remember getting him some tennis shoes and a fan. He was appreciative and upbeat.

Kelly's struggle continues — with his past, his incarceration, his future and his faith. In one of his many letters to me, he wrote, "I try everyday to give more of my situations to God, but in honesty it's not too easy. When I'm alone I talk with God, but when I get into different things it seems that I forget to turn my will over. I guess the more I practice the more I'll be able."

More recently, Kelly sunk into depression and pondered suicide. His latest letter, however, shows signs of hope. In addition to saying he wished he had met someone like me when he was a kid — another sign of his lifelong search for unconditional love — he wrote about his renewed strength.

> I have really learned my lesson this time, since I won't be using drugs anymore it's time to grow up and that I have been doing. I don't desire to kill myself any longer. I want to contribute something to life, I don't know my path yet but I am willing to do the right thing.
>
> . . . I have never hurt anyone, I just stole a lot to feed my habits, which all I was trying to do is get rid of the pain of being alone . . .
>
> The big message that I have learned from all of this is summed up in Matthew 5, 6 and 7, to be real with everyone, that is my goal for life. A number of things have contributed to this new person I am becoming; my mistakes were all centered around me trying to get away from life, but now I want to be a part of something real. My being screams for change.

The late Mother Theresa of Calcutta once said, "One of the worst diseases is to be nobody to nobody." In her book, *A Simple Path*, she writes, "The greatest disease in the West today isn't tuberculosis or leprosy, it is being unwanted, unloved, and uncared for. There are many in the world who are dying for a piece of bread, but there are many more dying for a little bit of love. . . . The poverty in the West is a different kind of poverty. It is not only a poverty of loneliness but also of spirituality. There is a hunger for love as there is a hunger for God. There is no substitute for love, there is no substitute for the transforming power of God's love. Somebody just has to be around long enough to show it's real."

Inmates like Kelly have been prisoners of an upbringing devoid of love, caring and support. God and religion are rarely seen as refuge when, as Mother Theresa puts it, no one "is around long enough to show it's real."

Many times their self-destructive behavior is simply a reaction to the pain and confusion of feeling "unwanted, unloved, and uncared for." Drugs and alcohol become a medicinal escape, gangs become a search for belonging and crime becomes a means of survival.

Like any learned behavior, a child who is a victim of or a witness to physical abuse is likely to view themselves as a deserving casualty or a rightful administer of punishment.

In the case of Jerry, an inmate I have known and corresponded with for 12 years, the damage to his identity eventually far outweighed the early physical abuse he suffered.

As a boy of age nine, a day I will never forget is the day when my mom actually picked me up (I was very small and skinny at nine) and threw me through the living room door, because she gave up caring about me as her child. On impact with the door and the outside ground, I broke my right wrist and two toes on my left foot, but I managed to pick myself up and I remember crying as I walked away. I still remember, because when your mom stops her love it's not something you forget as a child or a young man so easily, and I was not emotionally prepared at that young age to go through life all alone.

Although Jerry regularly attended our prayer services during his time at Cook County, for more than a year he never said a word to me or shared with the group. He'd sit near the back, his long, blonde hair neatly brushed, but his face, as I remember it now, was a disturbing picture of rejection, neglect and abuse.

From the age of nine, it was only a matter of time before I found my way to the prison system as a man. I had no help or guidance while growing up . . . and there was a lot about life and living that I didn't know or learn along the way. My mother threw me out of her life and onto the street, and from there the State and a few relatives from Georgia raised me. It has been years since I saw my mom or anyone from my family and I don't miss them because they put me out . . . and they never wanted to be a part of my life. But as a boy and a young man I wanted my mom and I wanted her to be a part of my life and I wanted to be a part of her life and I wanted to grow up with my family; and when this was not allowed to happen for me, I had a hard time of dealing with the feelings I felt in my heart.

It was not until Jerry opened up to God and joined the substance abuse program that he began to tear down the barriers he had constructed around him, the barriers that held his anger in and kept him isolated from others. In expressing himself to those in the drug program, he became far more comfortable with me and asked if we could meet alone. That is when I first learned his story.

For years I turned to drinking to hide my emotional feelings and problems, but these actions caused me even more problems with life and friends and knowing how to live with myself. During those years I was very much ashamed of who I was, and I was ashamed to have any person find out that my mom and family didn't love me. Rejection by your family has a way of making a person feel things that are not true. After not receiving the care, happiness, concern, support, attention, understanding and love by my family that all young people deserve while growing up, I took my anger of rejection, neglect, abuse, hurt feelings of loneliness, and abandonment out on myself, my friends and anybody who I thought was in my way.

I had no peace from my sinful actions and I never took any time for myself to just think about what I had become and what I was doing to myself and others in life. It was not right and in my heart I am truly sorry, but I took my problems out on friends and other people and I caused them great pain and suffering and misery. I was out of control because I had no understanding of myself, my feelings, of life and living, and of other people's feelings and these are the reasons for my incarceration in prison today. These reasons gave me no right to do what I did wrong to other people, because I am responsible for my actions and for being here on this day.

Jerry is now 40 years old and anxiously looking forward to his release date of June 27, 1999. He is a very intelligent man who, through his own search for understanding of himself, has reached out to other inmates and aided them both financially and through his sage counseling. In backing up his own advice, he has completed a GED program and taken several computer courses in prison.

Jerry's ambition in life is to keep close to the Lord and to learn as much as possible so as to be self supporting in a world he has not been an active member of for so long. I am convinced that Jerry will make a successful comeback to society although he, at times, has misgivings of whether he can do so. I continue to reiterate to Jerry that he must forgive his mother, and himself, if he wants to move on in peace.

This time called life is far more sacred and special than any of us can ever imagine, but before I will ever be able to participate in life, I have to first learn to deal with my guilt in a positive way, and I have enough of it to last a lifetime.

At times I can feel guilty about most anything — being in prison, causing trouble in my past, being rejected as a boy, and having emotional problems. But feeling guilty about my past benefits nobody, and I need to do any positive thing I can to let go of it. I am who I am. The past is just that, the past. I can choose freedom of thought and move on to a more positive way of life.

. . . I've gone through many mental and physical changes that are for the better, and as I continue to learn from the positive side of life, I realize that it not only lessens my emotional problems but increases my ability to be joyful in the midst of these prison walls.

Acceptance means that I can stop avoiding myself and start leaning into every situation surrounding my life. Despite my inability to control most things that go on in here, God gave me the gift of being free to respond to every situation in a positive and productive way.

With an open mind and an understanding heart, I accept the process of life and what it still might hold for me, and I'm praying and hoping for the very best.

Each human wants to love and be loved. If deprived of love, we are all tempted to turn toward destructive behavior. The addictions and abuses that take hold of us are not limited to drugs, alcohol and crime, but also power and wealth. They are avenues in which we look to satisfy our craving for love.

Only through faith can we stave off the temptation to replace love with reckless pleasures and material comforts. Our hearts are made for God and they will always be restless until they rest in Him.

Before stepping on to the elevator, Sister looks back at the cell doors that hold the patients of Cermak hospital. The elderly man in the hospital gown can still be seen wandering down the hall, his voice rising in song. A uniformed guard at the security desk reads a newspaper and slowly shakes his head.

4

Learning to Love

Sister carefully steps on the elevator and pushes the button marked "1." The doors slowly slide closed and she glances down at her watch. She peeks inside one of the bags she carries as the doors begin to open.

"How old are you? You look like a kid," she says, her piercing brown eyes focused on an inmate who stands just outside the elevator. The short, baby-faced man looks surprised at the sight of Sister Josephine emerging from the elevator. "Twenty-three," he eventually answers her, his brown wavy hair falling into his eyes.

Continuing the interrogation, Sister takes another step toward him and asks, "Is this your first time in here?" "No," he responds awkwardly, his feet shifting back and forth. "Do you like coming here?" she baits him. He drops his head and she scolds, "Well, you must if you keep coming back."

Before he can explain his circumstance Sister is moving down the hallway toward the security checkpoint. Perhaps sensing his distress, Sister turns her head back toward him without losing stride. "I'm sorry, but I must begin preparing for the prayer service," she calls to him. "Are you coming?"

"Yes, Sister," he replies. She smiles at him and marches on.

Although the judicial system is rarely thought of any longer as a rehabilitative institution, Sister Josephine claims being witness to

*progress in her own work. She has said she sees it in the inmates'
eyes, their faces and their behavior. She believes inmates become
more at peace with themselves when they realize they control their
own actions. She contends that if this approach toward a change in
attitude and outlook were as much a part of prison life as the concern with administering punishment, the rate of recidivism in this
country would gradually decline.*

In my ministry, I have witnessed inmates who have been
very responsive to love, understanding and discipline. I have
tried to reassure them that love, understanding and discipline
spell happiness, and that these things can only be found through
a spiritual realization of God.

Many of the inmates I've worked with have had very few
role models of true Christian living. Many expressed to me their
reluctance to go to any church services that condemned them
and ultimately reinforced their own worthlessness. Some were
only acquainted with a fire-and-brimstone god, a god that they
felt could only find fault with them.

God loves you very much, I would assure them. But this was
often met with the response that God cannot love me with all my
sins and crimes, with all the pain I've caused. I would remind
them that Jesus — sinless though He was — had been put in
prison and died for us. "I came not for the righteous, but for sinners," Jesus said.

This concept of unconditional love was mind-boggling to
many of the men. For them, revenge was the natural answer to
conflict. To turn the other cheek was not what many of them
thought of as the manly thing to do. But it is the Godly thing to
do. This was very difficult for many of the men to accept, that to
be loved you must accept love and express love. I would tell them
if you want to change your life or help change the life of another,
live out the spiritual principles of love. As Mother Theresa once
declared, "Love for God is love in action."

Like anyone else, inmates who begin to experience the positive effects of doing good feel the soothing waves of relief and

recovery. They need a constant assurance of God's love and forgiveness to realize they hold the key that opens the door to freedom, success and happiness — not the freedom, success and happiness described in our human world, but in God's everlasting world.

An inmate named Stanley put it best when he wrote, "Fortunately, I know God loves me just as I am, but in repentance I must change my heart and turn from this evil. The Holy Spirit is guiding me and is the only reason I am continuing to try in my therapy, even though it is so much easier just to give up . . . "

Sister Josephine has said she travels to the jail precisely to bring God and His love to men like Stanley, to introduce His love to those who have never experienced it or re-introduce it to those who never quite understood it.

A good number of the inmates Sister has worked with were exposed to some form of religious practice early in their lives. But being exposed to religion, she says, is not the same as experiencing God's love. For those whose childhood included some form of abuse — emotional, physical, sexual, etc. — Sister says it is likely they were unable to comprehend God's love in the midst of their painful reality. This powerful contradiction impeded their concept of love, and, therefore, their faith in themselves, other people and God. Still, only in finding their way back to God, she claims, will those inmates be at peace with themselves and those who have hurt them.

I believe that where you put love, you will find it. I believe that when a prisoner truly finds God to the point where he or she is on speaking terms with Him, in time their lives can and do change.

Tom is an example of one who has been vigilant in working to understand the wounds he has suffered and the pain he has inflicted.

I was blessed in birth by having a very devout Catholic mother . . . although my dad was an alcoholic and not one to express the love that a child seeks. My grandmother was a devout church-going Baptist. She disliked Catholics and especially their marriage rules in mixed marriages. My grandmother also sexually abused me from as long as I can remember until I went to the seminary at thirteen years old.

Mass and sitting in church became my escape. I would go to church at 6 a.m. everyday and stay until Dad went to work at 7:30 a.m. — not the ideal motive for attending Mass. However, I was only six years old and there was no escape from Grandma.

I repeated my sexual abuse on so many 12-year-old boys, refusing to admit it was wrong, or to take advantage of professional help offered. Just after my fiftieth birthday, I was convicted and given life in prison.

Tom is the father of three and became a grandfather for the first time while incarcerated. In the more than ten years he has spent in prison, I have received dozens of letters from him accepting responsibility for his crimes and seeking forgiveness from God, his family, his victims and himself. He continues to struggle with the human need for love and affection and the damage that such desires have caused him and others.

Many men [in prison] cope by selling themselves, teasing you once they know your vulnerable 'thorn in the flesh,' or entrapping you through manipulation of friendship. Discernment becomes a daily challenge. Only through surrender to the Holy Spirit can we sinful mankind succeed in not falling to such an overpowering human weakness . . . perhaps even human need. I have been successful in this necessary discernment, but I have not been alone. The Holy Spirit is my source, and my commitment remains strong . . .

I will never be around boys again — a blessing for the boys and me. I have worked through much of my trauma . . . and have confronted the serious trauma I have caused so many boys — much too much damage for me to ever know. I am taking the steps necessary to make sure I have no more victims. . . . Many will never be able to forgive me. I am sorry for all the horrible behavior I've done. I pray each day for my victims.

As for my grandmother . . . recovery deals with feeling and the pain and looking at the damage so as to understand and see the damage I've done. Of course, I have forgiven my grandmother and am in the process of forgiving myself.

As Tom has said, his healing "is a life-long process." He chooses to no longer see himself as either a victim or a victimizer, but as a child of God with a duty to live each day and face each obstacle with the same strength and grace represented in the life of Jesus.

Each inmate of the prison system receives $39 from the state each month, which is kept in a money order account that inmates may access in order to purchase food, soap, shampoo and other basic essentials from the jail or prison commissary. For several years now, Tom has forwarded his check to Sister Josephine with the intent that it be used to purchase the materials of her ministry. This is one of the few ways, according to Tom, of making some sort of reparation for his crimes. In accepting his charitable contribution, Sister Josephine says she is acknowledging his act of repentance.

Tom has also made great efforts to help his fellow inmates discover the hope and peace of accepting God's love. He has led Bible study groups and prayer sessions. And, he has attempted to share with others the hard lessons he has learned.

If you are someone who feels sexual urges toward children, seek professional help as early as possible, certainly today. If I had taken advantage of offered help at the age of 21, then many youth would not be suffering such mental trauma and other damages.

To young people, don't keep secrets of adult behavior that affects you. If you have been molested, tell until someone believes you, then get help from a therapist . . . and ask God to guide your recovery. Change those messages that [people like me] have distorted upon your mind.

To those in authority, if you suspect someone working with children, do whatever necessary to remove this person from working or being around children. Then, do whatever is necessary to get them professional help. The illness escalates and the damages become more traumatic.

Tom has been blessed with a family willing to work toward forgiveness and an understanding of his illness, despite the pain he has caused them. Because of their own Christian faith, they are also mindful that he is a child of God, a child who will die in prison.

There can be no love of God without genuine forgiveness. Forgiveness simply means that we forgive those who have hurt us, and wish them no harm. It does not mean we have to be with them all the time or say that what they are doing or have done is okay, because it isn't.

A superficial look at the world around us reveals the immense need for forgiveness rooted in the love of God. Without the gift of genuine forgiveness, those problems will continue to produce an ever-deepening atmosphere of guilt, isolation and hatred. At any moment we can turn to God and know there's love and forgiveness. It is often blame that stands in the way of faith and forgiveness. Rather than blame, we must repent.

Everyday we are called to love everyone around us: at home, in our workplace and even in prison. As St. Frances Cabrini said, "Today love cannot be hidden, it must become operative, living and true."

My dad is now so concerned about my wake and that I will be waked properly. Dad bought a lot and has my tombstone already up (a rosary adorns it as he knows my love for the Blessed Mother). Dad has paid mortuary and bought a casket, made arrangements with a church and a priest. He even has plans for songs and service. . . . Dad is showing me love as he knows how. I'm very blessed in him.

. . . The rest of my life is to be in prison, not a good place. Yet, as I accept my earthly punishment for such horrible damage I caused — and the minds I have permanently damaged — there is a Spiritual forgiveness which has led me to forgive those who have damaged me.

. . . I talk to God now in meditation. I accept each happening each day as part of God's plan, and I remember when things aren't going so well, that this too shall pass. Only God doesn't pass . . . and I am God's child.

I continue to correspond with Tom. He has told me he loves me and he knows my love is returned. I constantly remind myself that it is not up to us, we are not the ones who change things, God does. We are merely witnesses. But giving witness is not a passive response to the Gospel or without its demands. God never gives up on us and sends people, His ministers, in to jails and prisons and to parishes to convey this message. God's unselfish love is everlasting.

We cannot merit God's love, only accept and practice it. It is a free gift which we receive and allow to change our lives. God loves us for who we are, not for what we do. He knows everything we have done and will ever do. He loves us so much that He gave His only son to redeem us. He calls us His sons and daughters, and longs to shower us with a love that no earthly father could give. Let us receive this love so that we can give it to others.

St. Paul writes in First Corinthians 13: "I may speak the many languages of men and even of angels, but if I do so without love, my speech is no more than a noisy gong or a clanging bell. I may have faith enough to move mountains, but without love I am nothing. I may offer everything I own and even my body to be buried, but without love it does me no good. Love is patient and kind, not jealous or proud. Love is not ill-mannered, selfish or irritable. It keeps no record of wrongs. Love is not content with evil, but delights in the truth. Love never gives up. Its faith, hope and patience never fail."

My good friend, Father Armand Nigro, S.J., has said, "All these concerns, anxieties and fears stop us from loving. They lead us to close in on ourselves and impede us in our opening up toward God and doing His work, and opening up toward our neighbors and making ourselves one with them in order to love them as we should. We need, therefore, to abandon a purely human way of living in order to embrace a supernatural, divine love."

I minister at the jail because I have always loved those who are having difficulty. I have tried to see the inmates as God sees them — as His precious children — not as animals in a cage. I have attempted, by my actions more than words, to show that I love them with God's love. It is He who affects change, and we who are asked to cooperate.

Still, many inmates say, I can't believe that God loves me, sinner that I am, with all the evil that I've done. I encourage them to get to know God and believe that He loves them, to remember again what Jesus said, "I have not come in to the world for the just, but for sinners."

An inmate named Manuel — whom I ministered to for more than 12 years — wrote to me many times about his need to understand what place love has in the world, and how selfishness and neglect have kept him from the acceptance of love. He eventually concluded that love is the most natural of emotions, that love is the foundation of every emotion.

The key to love is the realization that expressing love is natural. True love is effortless. It is as natural and effortless as the sun rising in the morning or water seeking its own level. If there is effort to be expended, it is not in loving, but in releasing any unnatural behaviors and beliefs that do not allow us to do what is natural. The loving people of the earth do not strive to love, they strive to be what they are. With this comes love's expression.

The commandment, "Love one another," should be our heart's desire. We should want to love other people, even those who may dislike us. There is something inside us that tells us love is possible, that love is the natural order of things.

A good way to start knowing God is to start loving selflessly. Be there for one another, listen completely to one another, without interrupting, without feeling the need to fix whatever is wrong with the other person's life. Loving others can also be expressed by being positive in your comments, finding the right kind words that say, "I care," or doing something for someone else without need for recognition or gratitude.

We all struggle with this at different times in our lives. One inmate recently shared his current state. "There are moments when I wonder why being a Christian is so difficult and why God appears as an idiom at times. I continue to look ahead, no matter how difficult it may be at times. I know at some point I will be resuscitated by Our Holy Father and all which seems so perplexing now will once again be visible."

Another inmate wrote: "To love everyone without understanding them, I know this is possible. You are my role model for this. I have many difficulties with this though. It seems when I do get a little peace in my heart someone snatches it away. I really don't understand how to keep it."

If we look at Jesus we can observe that He loved His neighbor by feeding, healing, and giving. That, however, was not all He did. In order to love His neighbors perfectly and completely, He suffered and offered His life for them. When we suffer, Jesus is in our midst, proving that through strength and grace we will see the value of our suffering.

Father Pedro Arrupe, S.J., the former Superior General of Jesuits, has written: "What you are in love with, what seizes your imagination, will effect everything in your life. It will determine what will get you out of bed in the morning, what you will do with your evening, how you spend your weekend, what you read, who you know, what breaks your heart, and what amazes you with joy and gratitude. Fall in love, stay in love, and let love guide your every action."

Tom has written, "Pray I stay inside God's plan for my life, one day at a time, into and including eternity. The love of God is so deep and sincere, even in our darkest moments. God works in God's ways, not ours. Praise God for that."

This is not to say God's love admonishes our every action. As in Tom's case, part of accepting God's love is the act of accepting our misdeeds. In my ministry I have been careful not to betray my service to the inmates by excusing their behavior and actions when I am convinced they are at fault. In spite of everything, I love them dearly. But my approach with many of them has been one of "tough love."

For example, those who come regularly to the prayer services know I don't tolerate talking from those who see this time as a chance to socialize with friends. In the early days of my ministry, I was forced to ask certain people to leave if they insisted on talking. Soon after, the inmates began policing themselves and I rarely had to worry about a disruptive source.

When an inmate tells me something or denies guilt, I tell him I believe him because a lie would only do harm to himself. Often, those same inmates will come to me the next week and confess the truth. That is one mighty step toward love.

One inmate came to me and said he needed to talk to me in private because he needed to tell me something no one else knew. When we found a quiet place he said, "I am here in jail for having stolen, but that is not my greatest crime. When I lived in Puerto Rico I was struggling to put food on the table for my family." He went on to tell me that a very rich man offered to hire him to kill someone who was in his way. "I accepted," the inmate confessed to me. "I killed that man, took the money and eventually brought my family to the United States. When I arrived here I had very little money left and the little I had went fast, so I finally reverted to stealing and this is what's landed me here."

I told this man I was not a priest and could not absolve his sin. I told him to pray to God, to confess to the Father. He came back a week later and said he had thought and prayed about what he had done and could no longer keep quiet about it. He told me he had discussed this with his wife before coming to a decision. "I have decided to confess. My conscience will not let me live with this unless I return to my country and pay for my crime. After I serve my time here I will return to Puerto Rico and turn myself in."

When our insecurity and selfishness rule, we gravitate toward escape, self-destruction or the kind of control that only God possesses. One inmate had no trouble telling me that he wanted his wife to tremble when he spoke. I was shocked at his selfish arrogance and his need for power and control. I told him he does not own his wife. "You have equal privileges," I said. "God is the head of the family. Let God lead you in love and you will not feel the need for power and control."

This inmate looked at me as if I did not understand. He told me it was not that he did not love his wife, he told me she was a very good person and was a wonderful mother to their children. I interrupted him, saying, "And that's how you pay her back?"

When the man told me his wife wants to divorce him, I told him that came as no surprise to me, that if I were she I probably would have divorced him years ago. I told him that his quest for power might be an attempt to make up for his insecure feelings about God and God's love. Your insecurities, I said, may be driving your wife away from you. Seek out God's love and He will show you the way. This man acted as if I had hurt his feelings, but I told him this was a lesson in "tough love" that he ought to take some time to reflect on.

When I asked another inmate what his ambition was, he told me he wanted to be a professional thief. He wanted to learn how to get away with his crimes of stealing. I asked him if he felt such shame for himself that he would steal from other people. I told him, "It's one thing to be weak and desperate and steal, but another thing to intentionally learn how to steal so you can take from others." He told me he did not steal from people, that he was in jail for stealing from a railroad boxcar. We talked about the logic of his excuse and his ambition for some time. I do believe he will eventually be enlightened and take a more positive approach to his life.

A couple of inmates seemed to require constant attention from me, expressing severe sadness and disappointment when their letters weren't met with my prompt reply. I would reiterate my love for each one of them, but firmly explain that my delay in responding had to do with my responsibilities to others as well.

Others have attempted to con me, but I am quick to thwart their deception. For those inmates I have come to know well, I have made a habit of sending a card and $10 on their birthday and at Christmas and Easter. Very few have taken advantage of this practice, but some could not help but write me a laundry list of their need for more money. I explain to them that my friendship does not include being their financial source. They are usually embarrassed and apologize for their solicitation. When dire need for some assistance arises, I have made exceptions to certain inmates, and many have returned my favor in kind.

Chris was one inmate I eventually severed ties with. He was not in jail very long. When he was released a friend allowed him to stay at his apartment. The first night Chris stayed there he left his things in a room. He went out during the day and when he returned, he claimed, all of his things were missing. He called me late in the evening and told me of his problem, and asked if he could have some money in order to pay for a bus ticket to Florida. I gave it to him and a few hours later he called again, saying he needed more. I told him I could no longer help him financially. He promised to pay me back but I never heard from him again. I hope he is finding some peace and love from his parents, who, he says, were divorced after learning he is gay.

Tough love was also an approach I relied on in my many discussions and correspondences with Robert. Like Tom, he experienced abuse in his childhood. Robert's mother was a devout Catholic who took him to Mass, made sure he was confirmed and then received Holy Communion. But his introduction to the Catholic faith did not last. His early concept of love was distorted by the physical abuse his father commanded over him, and again by the selfish pursuits of those around him. This led Robert down a path away from the church and his family and toward his own self ruin.

> This life of corruption began in my life when I was about fourteen years old. I became so tired of living with the ridicule and beatings that I kept sleeping at my older sister's house. She had three children and was divorced. I would help her and she was like a protector to me. She prevented a lot of beating from my dad and, in turn, I would watch her kids at night.
>
> She was a wild woman. She would come home late at night and her friends would drink whiskey and smoke pot all night. I was like a butler to them. Any time they needed something, I would serve them. It was a lot better than being punched and whipped with a strap or pushed down a flight of stairs.
>
> Soon my lovely sister had me stealing from stores for her. She would stack all kinds of things in my arms and tell me to walk out of the store, and that if anyone stopped me I was to say I was lost and looking for my mother. . . . Soon she was showing me how to drink booze and smoke pot.

Robert bounced around from his sister's house, his parents house, and the apartments of other friends, but he never stayed in one place too long as he felt, "they controlled me too much for their selfish needs." Robert felt more comfortable around his cousins and others his own age, but his tendency to blame reached them as well. He says it was his cousins who furthered his involvement in crime and drugs.

> I would steal anything and everything I could to get money because the drugs were the most important things in my life. Besides, when I was high I didn't think about the neglect and pain I was feeling. Yes, I was a street tramp, and did just about anything for money.
>
> There was a time I was picked up by this man. . . . He took me to this construction building, and when we went

into this place, there were locked gates everywhere. I was leery and asked why the locked gates. He told me that the neighborhood was bad and the gates were locked for protection. We went into this elevator and it even had a locked gate. As we got into it he locked the gate and that made me very uncomfortable. When the elevator stopped on the floor we got off at, he locked that gate too. We went into an office and there were all kinds of blueprints and tools laying around. At first he was nice, but when I refused to let him sodomize me, he tried to handcuff me by pushing my face down on a wooden desk.

I managed to get a hand free and picked up a steel bar that was on the desk. I started swinging it at him, and kept screaming for him to keep his hands off me. At first he didn't care, but when he realized I wasn't playing, he gave up. I made him give me the keys and I kept that bar raised overhead until we were out of that place. Years later I found that person to be John Wayne Gacy. Just writing about this situation makes me shake. I still remember that day and it's been almost 20 years.

I never reported that incident to anyone for fear of being labeled a fag, but I wish I had. Maybe so many wouldn't have died. I lived with the pain for so long. I would use that experience as well as others for an excuse to drink and use drugs.

Robert has been incarcerated more than once. While he was in prison most recently, for 14 years, he learned of his father's death and the death of his wife, with whom he had a son. In his letters to me he shared his good times and bad, and told me he was seeking solace in the Lord.

He also told me how well he was doing in the classes he was enrolled in, and he shared his hope of beginning again with his son once he was released. He shared with me a painful letter he received from his son, who wondered why he couldn't be like other fathers instead of doing drugs and going to jail. Upon confirmation that he would retain custody of his son when he was released, Robert admitted his fear of failure. "I don't even know how to be a father," he wrote.

Robert told me of a girl he'd met through a friend and sought my advice on whether I thought she might be a good influence on him. He was not surprised, when I encouraged him to concentrate on forming a healthy relationship with his son. When Robert was released he was reunited with his son but also furthered his relationship with the woman he had met. Although I lost touch with him for some time after his release, I learned that his relationship with the woman did not work out.

For a time, Robert lived with his son in a trailer home somewhere in rural Illinois. He wrote to me in concern but was hopeful he could find another home for them so his son could attend school. I recently learned that Robert's struggles continue, and I pray that he will learn to take care of himself and his son.

Robert's painful past — his relationship with his father and other family members and his dependency on drugs — still seems to haunt him, both challenging his weaknesses and testing his faith. When he visited me at the hospital not long ago, I asked if he had been attending church. He told me he didn't need to go to church, "I make my home the church," was the excuse he used.

Years ago, when I visited Robert in prison and he was full of such pain and confusion I asked him to try to take all of his concerns about his family, his son and his drug problem and imagine putting them into the most beautiful box wrapped with a velvet ribbon. I told him to direct it to the Sacred Heart with this message: "Jesus, please take care of all these concerns and these dear people for I feel helpless and unable to do so." I remember how good he felt in doing that. He even advocated it to other inmates. I hope he'll think to do that today, to offer up his concerns to God and be strengthened by the power that comes with accepting His love.

I am sad to say that some inmates spend much of their time in jail reading the Bible and praying for their release or for a short sentence. When they feel their prayers have been heard, it is good-bye God until His help is needed again. Many inmates are released and feel no need to practice their faith because they have convinced themselves they already know God. They deprive themselves not only of an ongoing relationship with God that can be applied to their everyday life, but of a religious community that could be instrumental in providing the support needed to help in their continued rehabilitation. Thank God many of them eventually realize their plight and return to the church looking for more than just a casual relationship with God.

I realize there are many with whom I have come in contact who may never see the malignancy of their ways, understand the root of their behavior or find the strength to forgive and be forgiven. But, in God's name we must try. Of all the words Jesus spoke, none are easier to understand nor harder to practice than those involving forgiveness. In Matthew 18:21–35, Jesus clearly states that when our brother wrongs us we must forgive him not seven times, but, "seventy times seven times."

Heartened by these words, we must find the courage to view convicted criminals as our brothers and sisters. We must also recognize in them not only their diseased state but the divine origins we share with them. We have to work with prisoners. Discipline alone won't change anyone. You can only change someone through love.

5

❧

Enduring on the Inside

It is close to noon and officers have yet to announce Sister Josephine's 1:30 p.m. prayer service over the public address system. Because of the activities that inmates must participate in through-out the day — periodic inmate counts, doctor visits, meetings with attorneys, academic classes and substance abuse sessions — Sister worries that many will not be given the advanced warning needed to seek permission to attend her prayer service. While she sympathizes with their strict loyalty to procedure, Sister believes the lack of cooperation she sometimes receives from officers is not always accidental.

Before Sister can even utter her complaint, an officer at the security checkpoint on the first floor apologizes for the delay. "We're still waiting for the other officers to return from lunch," he says. "This has to be announced by the next shift."

Sister claims certain officers would rather not be bothered by what they may deem as her intrusion into the jail, but her ministry has always overcome such obstacles.

Besides being accused of giving an inmate a medal with which he later used in an attempt at suicide and tolerating comments such as the one from the officer who referred to the inmates as "animals" and suggested they need a bullet rather than confession, I've had a few other run-ins with the officers of Cook County jail. But, I decided early on not to be swayed by those who chose to hinder my work.

Once, as my bags were being cleared through security, a guard asked if he could have some of the candy that I had brought for the men. I offered him a handful just to stay on his good side, but I was insulted that a salaried employee would take from the little I had gathered for inmates who don't get regular treats.

Another time, because of a change in my schedule, I had to visit the jail on a Wednesday instead of a Thursday. When I got to the recreation room, where I hold the prayer services, there were officers playing pool on two pool tables at the back of the room. When these pool tables arrived weeks before, I was told they were for the inmates to use, but I had yet to see anyone but officers playing pool.

On this day, I asked the officers if there were any activities today that would keep me from holding services in this room. They said no, but then refused to leave when I told them we were beginning the service. One of the officers then called the superintendent of the jail and after some time announced very sternly, "The superintendent wants to speak to you."

I interrupted the service and as I went to the phone I noticed some of the inmates were upset that I might be reprimanded. The superintendent told me I had disrupted the activities of the day and it was the officers responsibility to enforce the rules. I went back to the inmates with great difficulty and dismissed them early that day.

After praying for the officer who made the call, I met him in the hallway and asked why he didn't tell me he had a group using the room or explain to me that I could not use it that day. "Don't talk to me," he snarled. The superintendent later apologized for the incident and told me it wouldn't happen again.

About a year later, after being away from the jail for a few weeks in the summer, I was told by an officer that I could no longer use the recreation room for my prayer services. Besides the pool tables, the recreation room was equipped with benches and a podium and was fairly clean and spacious. The clothing room, where we were told to hold our services from then on, was rather small, lacked any real seating and certainly couldn't hold the 40 or more men that we were regularly drawing.

We decided to try it out and it was a disaster. Many men had to sit on dirty mattresses while others were forced to stand and, because it was the room where the inmates' street clothes are kept, inmates who were released or were due in court kept coming in and out to retrieve their clothing.

The following week I began setting up the recreation room for services and again the officers were playing on the pool tables. "Don't you understand you can't use this room?" one of them scolded me. I could not resist my sense of frustration and I told them, "All I ask is an hour with the inmates in peace, and if I can not have that I might as well go home." I threatened to call the superintendent this time, but they called instead. Thankfully, the superintendent told the officers to allow me use of the room and he would decide on a better solution later. I was never moved from that room again.

The Religious Freedom Restoration Act was passed in 1987. Prior to its passage, the U.S. Senate defeated an amendment which would have excluded prisons from application into the bill, meaning instead that offenders have greater access to legitimate religious practices.

Under the act, the courts are to be far less deferential toward religious restriction with the burden placed on the government to monitor and prevent impairment of such practices. This means a religious practice may not be arbitrarily denied, but can be denied on the basis of safety, health and the orderly running of the prison.

This act was interpreted by some officials to mean that they should limit each inmate to one religious practice per week. One inmate told me, "I don't go to the other religious services. I would like to but they will only allow me to go to one and I want to go to your service."

Overall, I have been blessed with little trouble in offering
inmates of Cook County religious services and counseling. There
have been many jail superintendents — wardens are those who
manage prisons rather than jails — who have been very supportive of my work and cooperative in allowing inmates the time to
see me. Some superintendents have even sought counseling for
themselves and their families. The same is true of many of the
officers who were approachable, appreciative and as cooperative
as they could be in a job that I am sure be can very stressful.

One outstanding superintendent of Division #8 was Captain John Morris. He always made time to talk and was very good
with the inmates. He often referred me to specific inmates and
also referred inmates to me. "Sister, here's Andy," he would say.
"He is so wicked that you'd better exorcise him. He needs God in
his life very badly."

Captain Morris showed great compassion to many of the
inmates, and he was sorely missed when he was transferred to
the women's division. Through the letters of a few of the inmates
I have learned that Captain Morris is gradually losing his eye-
sight and can no longer work in the jail. He is in their prayers
and mine as well.

There are always human and systemic impediments involved when dealing with an especially delicate bureaucracy like
that of the correctional system. Despite the many times we were
successful, it was always very difficult to get permission to have a
priest come into the jail to say a Mass, perform a Baptism or hear
Confessions. At one point I organized a three-hour retreat for
the men but there were so many permissions to be granted and
logistics to overcome that it was impossible to try again. When
we thought we finally had cleared all of the hurdles, we were reprimanded for allowing an inmate to operate a disposable camera.

These little frustrations, however, are nothing compared to
the everyday restrictions the inmates are forced to abide by. Certainly, discipline is often what they need, and usually what they
crave. But, in jail or prison, rules and regulations can lead to
more than the loss of privileges. It can amount to the loss of
identity. As one inmate wrote:

Nobody here cares about anything, and they treat you like you should fall off the face of the earth. The worst of it is I don't blame them. They [the staff] are cold-hearted, which scares me because that's exactly how I've been feeling, very cold-hearted about the others who are around me. I know God is with me. It just makes things lonely. I don't have anybody to talk with about good, pure things. Instead people who surround me want to talk about stealing, or getting away with something . . .

In prison, your clothing differs only in the numbers printed across it. You are a number, not a name — many times I could not even find an inmate because I only had his name. In prison, you are taught to fear other inmates and authority. Gangs are prevalent, as many are either pressured to join or seek the protection of a gang. Rapes are another dysfunction of prison life. One inmate described his prison environment this way:

> I have never in my life felt so close to death and the grave until now. I try to think about something else so that feeling of death leaves me.
> I have been having problems with a certain gang member who is wearing out my patience. I might have to go to the prison's officials here about him . . .
> Each day I face these cold steel bars to leave my cage and out there, out there waiting for me is my reality. Individuals who are as confused as I am, some even helpless and many depressed and frightened. People exploding from the daily pressures that surround them are a daily occurrence; so is the bitterness that is released on one individual on another. It seems so animalistic and one wonders if it was premeditated or just the sickness of this decaying environment.

Unlike the jails, the population of penitentiaries does not dramatically fluctuate on a daily, weekly or even monthly basis. Security can be especially tight and the relationships among inmates and between inmates and guards can easily become strained. It is essentially a community where one group rules over the other, making the potential for violence ever present. One inmate described the ongoing problems at his penitentiary as a test of his faith in God.

> . . . This prison has been [on lock down] for over two weeks. Last week 13 inmates overdosed on drugs, one of them died, so the drug problem has gotten real bad. . . . God said those things would happen in the last days, and now is the time to truly get into the Spirit because when God washes away all the evilness in the world, the children of God, the true children of God will be saved.

An inmate on death row wrote me a series of letters when tensions ran high in the prison he called home.

> Nothing has changed here. The general populations is still on lock up since the shooting death of an inmate by a guard. A few weeks later a guard was stabbed in the neck and chest. It was said three guards would die for the taking of one life.
> . . . Two officers had to be taken to the hospital because one had hot water thrown on him and the other was set on fire. I'm just doing my best to stay out of it or anything else. My nerves are shot at this point and I just want to relax . . . and stay out of people's way.

Trust is not always something that serves you well in prison. Authorities use inmates to gather information about other inmates. Inmates share information in order to lessen their time in jail. One inmate told me he was offered the chance to reduce his sentence if he would testify against another inmate. The offer was tempting, he admitted, but he had no truthful information to pursue the deal.

Other inmates have felt the sting of a prison community that not only pits inmates against each other, but fuels the animosity of those in charge. One inmate told me of his dire attempt to seek work at the prison commissary:

> Those in power are preventing me from working. I have applied for six openings with no luck, some [of those openings] were filled by men just coming here. I have been told by a couple of staff that I am on a list not to hire. It has to do with a high official who is misinformed about some lies that were spread by inmates as they were angry at me. . . . I spent almost a month in confinement (segregation) until the warden herself discovered my presence there, investigated the charges, found me not guilty and freed me [from confinement]. This made certain officials even angrier and more determined to try to break me.

Some inmates cope with insubstantial or even wrongful convictions and an inadequate judicial system that keeps them in jail while their trial is delayed again and again. Another inmate told me the authorities wanted him to admit to a murder that he said he did not commit. He told me he would never do that, "They can keep me in prison the rest of my life but I will never admit to something I did not do."

Many inmates feel as if they must wear an emotional shield of armor as protection against the rigors of prison life. Often, however, the experience of prison leaves inmates yearning for the innate expression and experience of love. I found the following inmate testimonial in a prison newsletter.

"So You Want to Be a Tough Guy"
by Mark Verdi

> I've been outside maybe six times since I went to jail, and that's been in a concrete cube. I'd walk back and forth, and if I was lucky, I'd notice some grass in the cracks in the concrete. I wish I could feel grass again. Once I found a cricket in the courtyard and thought about bringing it to my cell but I didn't want it to be confined like me.

I can barely see out of my window, but I do see people rushing here and there. I wish I could be one of them or at least be able to shout to them to slow down and see what God has given them. I see couples holding hands and walking through the courtyard, oh how I envy them. I had that once but I was too tough to appreciate it.

Some days I put my cheek against the window trying to feel the warmth of the sun. Many nights I lay with my heart hurting because of what I've done to others.

When an inmate's family member dies, in most cases they are permitted to view the body if they are able to come up with $300 to cover the accompaniment cost of two guards. They are only permitted to view the body before the funeral, however, and without seeing any other family members.

In institutions where schooling opportunities are available, inmates can use their idle time constructively, rather than spending it watching the violence of most television shows. I believe if inmates receive an education in an institution, there is a much greater chance of them being rehabilitated by the time of their discharge. Not only do they feel better about themselves — for actually accomplishing something while incarcerated — but they are better equipped to succeed in society.

. . . Here are my intentions to occupy my time while I'm here. I hope to go back to school. I'd like to go back to college but possibly I'll take a vocational course in drafting. I think I mentioned to you that is the line of work my father is in. I've signed up for both classes, but I've heard all the classes are full because they give additional good time for going to school. I know my test scores were very high so maybe they will help me get into school.

I've got to be honest; I wouldn't mind some additional good time also. While I was at the school taking my tests, I inquired about tutoring. The teacher was happy I was interested in helping because it's on a volunteer basis. I'm scheduled to take a course for twelve hours to be a certified tutor.

Then I will begin helping others study for their GED or whatever they need help in. You know I really do enjoy helping other people any way I can. So that will keep me busy a few evenings.

School, however, is not an option for certain inmates. Those who are eligible often contend with a long waiting list, and varying opportunities depending on state law.

I'm a bit discouraged about school because the rumor is that this is the last semester offered, as the state is discontinuing all school programs except GED. I need only two more semesters to obtain my college degree. I'll remain optimistic until there is a final word.

The negative temptations of incarceration are immense; inmates are tempted to steal from each other, to lash out at each other and authority, to attempt suicide, or to simply lose themselves in their misery. It has been my experience that inmates who gravitate toward religious introspection and positive activities begin to support each other, protect each other, learn from each other and pray for each other.

Not only have many of the inmates I have worked with at the jail continued to correspond with me over the years, but those who passed through the jail together have also kept in touch with each other as best they could. Some were sent to the same penitentiary, where they looked to each other for comfort and support. Some who were released continued to write and call those who went on to prison. Others relied on me to update them on a friend who'd been sent elsewhere.

Through the prayer services I have attempted to create a sense of community among the inmates and encouraged them to do likewise by looking after each other in the jail. I have convinced inmates to share their stories, their pain, their fears and their hopes at each prayer service. I have also shared mine. Once, an inmate decided to sing his message at the prayer service and it made everyone's day. Through these gatherings, bonds were formed and a sense of optimism could be found in an atmosphere that tends to breed despair and hopelessness.

Sadly enough, even participating in negative activity in jail or prison is oftentimes just another way of searching for companionship and support. One inmate wrote to me about a friend attempting to avoid trouble with a gang. "It is a shame what Charles is going through. The gangs tried the same thing with me. It is good he refused to join their play of hurting people. I will make sure to include him in my prayers tonight."

One inmate wrote of his excitement to learn of a friend's transfer to the prison where he himself was being held.

> To my surprise, Scott arrived here a week before I did. I was so happy to see him. I'm really proud of him and his accomplishments over the past two years. What I really appreciate is the opportunity to have someone with whom to discuss serious issues — someone who can understand and give me feedback and vice versa . . .
>
> Scott is doing well. We see each other almost every day, have lunch or dinner together. It's nice to have him around. . . . After giving it some serious thought and prayer, I decided to tell him about my illness. Since I already feel better, I don't have to deal with it completely alone.
>
> . . . I'm a bit confused about Eddie. I've written him twice now and haven't heard anything from him. I hope he's doing okay. . . . If you should write him, please send him my regards.

Another inmate wrote to me to express his disappointment that a friend had been transferred to another prison; another wrote me in concern of a mutual friend and a third wrote of his gratitude of a new friendship he could rely on.

> My best friend was taken to a much worse prison setting — Menard Prison. I miss him, but thank God for the almost two years we shared. [He] was a blessing to me and encouraged me so in changing and growing spiritually. I

fear for his safety, but know he belongs to God . . . I continue to pray [for him].

Jim needs our prayers, Sister. He has gotten himself in much trouble here, which included a fight. It is a challenge in prison or elsewhere to resist trouble . . .

Jesus is sending me friends who do encourage me and I enjoy their company. One man lived in my city and went to school three blocks from our house and we know some of the same families.

He was at County, Division #8. He didn't go to services but says he knows you. He tells me he will never accept a gift from me and is going to show me I deserve a friend because of who I am, not what I give.

He is very simple in living, in having very little — one pair of pants, one shirt, one pair of socks and shoes falling off his feet — yet he gives anything and everything to those in need. He gives his time and a smile to those hardly anyone will speak to. He listens to me and shares his feelings with me . . .

Inmates released to society are given $30 to $50 which, for most inmates, is not even enough money to find their way home — if they have a home. Those who are lucky have family members willing to pick them up or who are at least awaiting their arrival.

One man, who was released after being incarcerated for over a decade, did have a family to go home to but found himself imprisoned by the bureaucracy even after his release. It was the middle of winter when he was released and provided with a pair of slacks, a short-sleeved t-shirt, a spring jacket and thirty dollars. He had planned to make his way home to Ohio from Illinois by bus but was told, as he was being freed, that he was not yet permitted to leave the state. The necessary paperwork had not yet been circulated to proper authorities.

This man made his way to Columbus Hospital on the city's north side in the midst of a snowstorm and had no choice but to spend his money on a hotel room. Luckily, his family was able to send him some money because it was not until two weeks later that he was legally free to return home.

Many times I have been told by those released how difficult it is to find an organization willing to help them in their transition to society. If being placed in a halfway house is not a condition of their discharge, they often find themselves with no money, few prospects for employment, alienation from family and friends and perhaps even a lack of shelter. With this re-introduction to society, they are left vulnerable to their former habits of survival.

Sister Josephine leans into the counter at the security checkpoint on the first floor, her face gliding closer to the uniformed man who slouches in a chair on the other side. "You promise me you won't forget to tell them," she says gently. Just as the officer nods his assurance Sister turns her attention to three uniformed guards who can be seen striding down the dank corridor of Division #8. "Here they come," Sister informs the seated officer.

"This is Sister Josephine," the man in the chair greets his fellow officers as they reach the security checkpoint. "Of course it is," replies the tallest of the three. "Yeh, well, you've gotta announce her service 'cause I'm outta here." He stands and pushes one arm into his black leather coat while his other arm pulls open a door at the side of the counter.

"Okay Sister, no problem," says the tall officer, "we just have to do a quick inmate count and then we'll let 'em all know." Sister looks up at the officer in disappointment. "Can't you announce it before the count?" she pleads. "Nope, not 'til afterwards, but it won't take but a few minutes and then we'll let 'em know loud and clear."

"Okay then, officer," Sister responds, "I'm going to begin setting up in the recreation room and you are going to announce the service as soon as the count is finished."

"That's right, Sister."

My friends often ask me, "Aren't you afraid to be around the jail filled with so many violent men and women?" In response, I tell them no one forces me to go. I feel no fear in going. In fact, many times the inmates themselves shield me from any potential danger. They support me in the same way they support each other.

One afternoon I was in one of the dormitories and a big, tall and sturdy inmate said to me, "Sister, do you see that man over there? He's the one who murdered that nun in her home. If he tries to put a hand on you, we're all here to defend you." I told him I had no fear, I was sure the man would do nothing to me, but the large man and a few other inmates stayed there just the same.

I did speak to this inmate, who was accused of murdering a nun, and asked him if he wanted anything. He said very little. All he wanted was cigarettes and candy. He actually came to a couple of prayer services, before being sent to prison.

I go to the jail because I have been called by God to this privileged ministry. I love each inmate and each officer with whom I have come in contact. Each morning during prayer, I ask Jesus to accompany me, to protect and inspire me. I've never felt fear in the jail. In everyone I meet I see Jesus present in them.

In addition to the inmates and several members of the staff, I have also been the recipient of the loving support of many volunteers to this ministry. Only through the encouragement, dedication and passion of these people have I been able to spend more than 14 years ministering to the inmates of Cook County — and those who have moved on to further incarceration.

In the early days of the ministry there was a team of about five volunteers and one priest. Because the correctional facility was largely uncooperative with our weekly group visits, many of those volunteers eventually moved on to other work.

Besides Sister Renee Kittleson, who introduced me to the ministry, I was blessed with the weekly accompaniment of Deacon Marv Kocar and his wife Peg. They were truly effective in relating with the inmates and in their help with the prayer services. During this time, we were able to invite inmates to participate by praying aloud, and by convincing inmates to write and say their own readings. After more than a year being by my side at the jail, the Kocars were called to undertake other ministries and have continued to be of great service to others.

Rev. Harry Mierose, S.J., was also a committed volunteer for quite some time. He came weekly to offer Mass, hear Confessions and minister to the inmates before being assigned to a Diocesan parish. Deacon Michael McClaskey and his wife, Debbie, joined me as often as they could — preparing inmate readings at the prayer services among many other things — before being called away as Debbie was named principal of a school in Chicago.

At one time I was in need of a priest for an inmate who was to receive the Sacraments and there was no Catholic chaplain at the jail. My friend, Mary Bottala, had met Father Stephen Kozinsky and invited him to come and help me in the ministry. I called him and he readily agreed to come and administer the Sacraments. He was gracious to come on such short notice and was also relied on at other times before being named associate pastor of a parish near his home.

Father Ted Ploplis was also a willing volunteer on occasions when we were in need of one to administer the Sacraments to an inmate. One Easter morning he called me and asked if I would like him to come and offer Easter Mass for the inmates after his tour of duty at our hospital. I was thrilled. We prepared everything for the Mass and the inmates were so surprised, pleased and happy. They made sure to show their appreciation to him.

Long-time volunteer Adele DeSanto, despite her full-time employment, made an effort to join me as much as she could. She took free days and even vacation days to help with the inmates and the prayer services. She often baked goodies and brought candy for the inmates and always offered a smile to those who needed a boost. Inmates often write to me asking about her and telling me how much they appreciated her time with them.

Various charismatic groups of Chicago have also made many trips to the jail with me and were of great help with our special events. With all of their musical instruments, it took one group at least a half hour to get through security to attend our Inmate Retreat days. With the ministry of word and music the retreat lasted only a few hours, but we were fortunate to have that little time with them.

I met volunteer Patty Kersey through Sister Renee. She joined Sister and me as we met with inmates being held on death row. A fairly recent convert to Catholicism, Patty is truly an evangelizer at heart. The connection she forged with inmates was astounding. She never failed to inspire the inmates with her expression of faith, and for that faith the Lord rewards her trust. She is now a teacher and also a leader of many ministries. She continues to work with those behind bars.

From time to time I corresponded with an inmate who was executed on November 19, 1997. In his letters, he always mentioned the kind and helpful letters he received from Eileen Bosshart. It was not until a few months before he was executed that I realized what a treasure she was to him and to others. Not only did she correspond and visit with this man, but for many years she served as a foster parent to severely disabled children. When this inmate was executed, she offered her burial plot. She also conducted a prayer service for him. Unfortunately, my poor health kept me from attending.

Sister Miriam Wilson was a member of the regular team that worked in different parts of Cook County jail. I was privileged to meet with her on many occasions. Sister volunteered for the Department of Corrections' Programmed Activities for Correction Education (PACE), and many Bible study programs. In 1982, the archdiocese appointed her Prison Chaplain at Cook County, where she ministered tirelessly to those on death row, inmates at the jail and their families and inmates of the Illinois prison system. This is what she wrote during these years: "I do a simple thing, I go to jail everyday. It has had a profound effect on my life and reaches deep into the understanding of our community. Since 1983, and after many years of teaching, I began a full-time pastoral presence at our County jail."

Sister Miriam fought for the rights of those in prison. She spent many long hours visiting prisoners, meeting with their families and going to court with them. She made long, exhausting trips to Springfield when a review board was in session to speak up for one or more prisoners on death row. She was for many years a very vocal member of the Illinois Coalition Against the Death Penalty. When a prisoner was to be executed, she stood with others outside the prison gates to pray. She contracted her last illness, pneumonia, and died almost three years ago.

Sister Miriam has been an incredible inspiration to me, as has Sister Antonia Brenner, who continues her work a world away from Chicago. I met Sister Antonia at a recent Marian Conference in Chicago. She was one of the presenters speaking of her prison ministry in Tijuana, Mexico. Sister had been married for many years and had seven children. When her children were grown she joined a religious order and started her remarkable ministry at age 50.

Living in a small cell in the prison, Sister Antonia is said to be able to control violent prisoners whom even the officers fear. A word from Sister Antonio is said to be law to them. She has been involved in this ministry for 20 years.

After her presentation in Chicago, Sister Antonia received a long standing ovation from the assembly. I made a point of meeting her briefly after the event. I greatly admire her.

Janet McNally is years younger than Sister Antonia, but no less of an inspiration. She is from England and recently completed her stint as a United Kingdom student, in which she joined the Cabrini Mission Corps. Much like the Peace Corps., students are asked to give a year or more of service at foreign and domestic sites.

With a background that includes work with drug abusers and an interest in criminal rehabilitation efforts, Janet immersed herself in the prison system of this country. At the end of their term, students are to make a presentation of their experience at the Cabrini Mission Conference. As I have been on the CMC Advisory Board for six years, I was present for Janet's report and have included this excerpt:

. . . When I first stepped into the prison, I realized I had entered a different culture where I would be scrutinized for the way I spoke, what I said, my body language, how I dressed, whom I talked to and for how long. Even the length of time you shake hands with someone means something in the prison environment.

Some inmates can still recall what I wore on my first day. As a young female in this environment, five days a week, I had to put up so many guards, and be 100 percent alert in my surroundings. This was a hard test, as I felt I was in a vulnerable space, in the process of a transition, away from my support network of valued family and friends. Although I had worked with offenders before, enclosed prison environment intensifies the predatory and manipulative elements of individuals . . .

It was hard again working in an environment where I was unsure of whom or what to trust, and what to fear and guard against. I only know that when I'm faced with this I want the purity and truth of God, some truth I could trust . . .

I accompanied one man on his eighth step of recovery, part of the twelve-step recovery program. This involved listening to all that he wanted to confess, to off load all those ugly things he'd done and was ashamed of, a real confession. These crimes filled me with an anger and disgust, a feeling of sordidness, and knowing I walked the corridors of a prison surrounded by this. I was able to sit within this, however, beside the person who had perpetrated such violation of another, and see only a person, a human before me, rather than his crime.

Many of the letters Sister Josephine has received from inmates over the years have included gifts of creativity. She's received dozens of religious drawings, paintings and sketches. One inmate always decorated the envelopes he addressed to Sister, and another once sent her a crucifix made of match sticks.

I sought the Lord, and he answered me, and Delivered me from all my Fears. Look to him, and be Radiant; So your Faces Shall never be ashamed.

The early days of the Cook County ministry included the team of: (from left to right) Sister Josephine, Peg Kocar, Sister Renee and Deacon Marv Kocar.

At a reception for ministry volunteers at the jail, Sister Josephine stands between dedicated volunteer Patty Kersey (right) and the late Sister Miriam.

Inmates relax before Sister's prayer service begins. In the background, Sister introduces herself to those who are attending for the first time.

The inmates stand for prayer at one of Sister's prayer services in the jail's recreation center.

December 17, 1993

Dear Sister Josephine:

I want to thank you for the beautiful Christmas card, and the ten dollars you sent. You do not know how much I appreciate this gift. The Lord seems to always bless me in the best ways. I also want to impress upon you how much I appreciate you coming to see me, and the Church service you held. I feel every time I talk to you, or attend one of your church services I come closer to the Lord. I hope my being in jail will not be your lasting first impression of me. I care for you, and want you to know, I hold my up~~utmost~~ grattitude for you. May God bless us all!

Love
Christopher
:)

Sister organized an Inmate Retreat Day, where inmates studied the Scripture, shared their stories and enjoyed a buffet lunch provided by volunteers.

Inmates Scott (left) and David first met at one of Sister's prayer services in Cook County jail. They were reunited later at a penitentiary in Southern Illinois. They took this picture in a prison classroom to show Sister they were both keeping up with their academic pursuits.

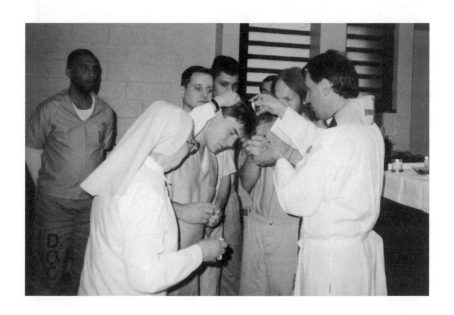

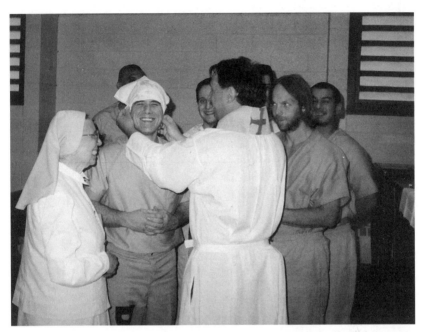

Sister Josephine has served as a sponsor to many inmates who have been Baptized at Cook County jail. Father Steve came all the way from Indiana to Baptize an inmate named Richard. Other participants of Sister's prayer services served as witnesses to this sacred event, which included more than a few light moments.

Sister and volunteer Patty Kersey visited death row inmates Jim (left) and Durlyn. They were both executed in 1997 for their crimes.

June 2, 1997

Dear Sr Josephine,

Thank you for the birthday card it
was beautiful.

Sorry I'm just getting back to you.

For a while I was just walking
around in my own world.

The pressure and tension was more
than I could bear it sort of caught me
off guard.

But I was able to regain my sense's
in time.

But I will say this I don't want
to go through that again because I
was hurting bad.

I put such a strain on my body I
felt like a giant Rubber band I was so
tight.

But I have moved on from that.

Well I hope your sister is doing
much better now.

And don't you worry because you're
always a part of me.

Sometimes life's like that time just
goes by so fast or you are just to

OVER

busy to do the things you enjoy.
I will keep you up to date on things
I love the music note's on the letter
Take care and God bless you.
                              Love
                              Jocelyn

Sister meets briefly with the inspiriting Sister Helen Prejean, author of the best-selling book, Dead Man Walking.

After accepting the Templeton Award, prison reform activist Chuck Colson takes time to meet with Sister Josephine.

your

FRIENDSHIP AND HELP

WILL ALWAYS BE DEAR

TO ME. MAY GOD BLESS

you!

an older inmate who joined the church

Happy Holidays,
Hyon Sufi~ Joe

11-19-89

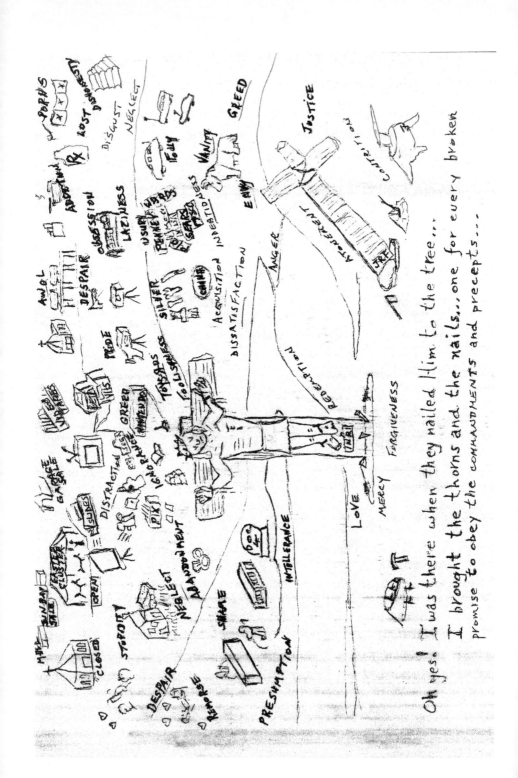

Oh yes! I was there when they nailed Him to the tree...
I brought the thorns and the nails...one for every broken
promise to obey the COMMANDMENTS and precepts...

6

Living on Death Row

Despite her many experiences with the inmates and officers of Division #8, Sister Josephine admits she was not prepared for what awaited her on her first visit to inmates on death row. Sister Renee Kittleson, who had introduced Sister Josephine to the prison ministry before being reassigned to a ministry in Seattle, returned to Chicago in 1988 for a visit with inmates she had first encountered at Cook County jail. One inmate she planned to visit was then being held on death row at Pontiac Correctional Center in Pontiac, Illinois. Sister Renee asked Sister Josephine if she'd like to come along.

Since 1976, the death penalty has taken the lives of 486 people. In that same period, no fewer than 75 people have been exonerated after being sent to death row. For every seven people executed in the last two decades, one condemned person has been cleared. Currently, 3,500 inmates remain on death row in this country.

I had been going to Cook County jail for seven years when Sister Renee invited me to join her. She was visiting a man named Charles whom she had continued to correspond with over the years. He was being held on death row for the 1980 Valentine's Day murder of his girlfriend and his girlfriend's sister.

Once inside the prison we were told to empty our pockets and were thoroughly searched for contraband. All excess items were placed in a locker to be retrieved after the visit.

We were escorted to another building where we received a stamp on our wrist. We were told to wait in a cafeteria-like room and, eventually, Charles arrived in handcuffs. We sat and ate the pizza that we had purchased at the prison commissary and Charles was quite adept at maneuvering his cuffed hands up to his mouth. For some time we talked freely about his fears and his faith. With Sister Renee's help, Charles was Baptized later that same year — he said it was "the day life really, really began for me." Charles was the first man I ever met who was sentenced to die. That day, I had trouble holding back my tears.

It was Sister Renee who first reached out to Charles after reading an article on his case in the *Chicago Sun-Times*. "I wondered why a nun wanted to write me," Charles was quoted as saying in the January 23, 1994, issue of *Catholic Times*. He said her letter sat with a pile of others in the corner of his cell but kept working its way up to the top of the stack. Sister visited him for the first time a short time later. "The first thing she did was grab me and hug me," he recalled. "My face sort of froze. . . . Here was a person I didn't even know, and she showed me the way."

The late Sister Miriam Wilson, whom I also mentioned previously, became a friend to Charles as well. But it has been his relationship with God that's helped him face each day. "God continually reminds one of mercy if one shows repentance. But we have to be sincere," he once said. "I not only [killed] two people, I hurt hundreds of other people unintentionally. Deep in my heart, I feel their pain. All I can do is pray for them."

In one of many letters to me, Charles expressed his genuine surrender to our Lord:

> You know I am very ecstatic about God's will and love and merciful grace and power over my life today and always. Why? Because He has showed me through miracles and His divine grace and love and the gifts of life He has willed me each day. Yes, I don't worry about myself, I worry

about the people around me that I love and cherish most, [I worry] how they feel and are doing about this thing that man said you will pay for. . . . When God is ready for me to come home to Him, He will call me there. Until then, why should I worry and cause myself and others hardship and pain?

. . . Sister Josephine, I wish I could walk from these walls and go and minister in the streets as Jesus did during His walk with man's ultimate plan for Him. He knew His time was short and what He was placed here to do, I could only hope to be part of the man Jesus was and is today.

Charles' gratitude to all who have tried to help him has been obvious throughout his incarceration. He once planned a surprise birthday party for Sister Renee at the prison. He invited all of the prison staff and chaplains and presented Sister with a sweater that was knitted by one of the inmates. He promised and later sent me a framed painting he made of the Mother of Jesus. It is beautiful. It was presented to our Superior General at our Provincial Assembly and she has since placed it in the shrine at Codogno, Italy — that so-called "Cradle of our Institute" — where the order's most meaningful documents are displayed. It bears the inscription, "Painted by Charles on Death Row, as a tribute to Mother Mary and Mother Cabrini." I wish Charles were able to see it there, but in its place his gratitude will always be remembered.

I can, however, share a poem Charles wrote from his cell. It's called "My Rose of Memory," and it's another example of his quest to find beauty in a place of true darkness.

There's a creeping red rose vining over my door,
With petals like velvet in clusters of four.
It sends out a fragrance of lovely perfume,
As all through the summer it hangs full of bloom.
Bright bees and butterflies swarm thick on its leaves,
And the gay little hummingbirds flit through the breeze.
It is really a picture of Nature in Rhyme,

And I watch my old creeper for hours at a time.
I have many flowers of bright color and hue,
That sparkle like gems when kissed by the dew.
But this cherished old creeper holds a place set apart,
For it weaves fondest memories deep down in my heart.

Charles has compared his own life with the bursting hues of a flower. "I was a late bloomer as the flower of God's creation and came alive when I made the decision to turn my life and my will over to God as I understand Him and love and cherish Him today and always, 'til long after this body is returned to the stage in which it started out."

Charles has already received one stay of execution, which has kept him alive longer than he once thought. He is still, however, expected to die by lethal injection. His hope is that his grave will be marked with a Veteran's bronze plate, as he served his country and was honorably discharged. But, more importantly, Charles has written, "As far as my needs, they are small and my wants are that the prayers from the sisterhood always be there for me and pray special prayers for me and my family and friends. . . . I will be buried with my cross and a rosary around my neck."

I also came to know a death row inmate named Durlyn, who was executed by lethal injection on November 19, 1997, for the 1977 rape and murder of a 9-year-old boy. I first started corresponding with him more than ten years ago. Dedicated volunteer Patty Kersey and I visited him shortly before the execution of Jim, another inmate at Pontiac Correctional Center. Jim also joined us in our visit and at that meeting Durlyn had trouble controlling his emotions.

Durlyn was a large, husky man who always seemed very sensitive. He admitted that most of his life he was uncomfortable showing his feelings. He later wrote me a letter explaining and almost apologizing for his tears that day. He said that during our visit he was overcome by the sincere kindness Patty had showed to Jim. "I realized that Patty was really concerned about [Jim] as a person," he wrote. "No pity or anything like that, she cared for him as if he was a part of her family. . . . That really touched me deep down inside."

Jim corresponded with Patty up until his very last days. In his last letter to her, he wrote:

> . . . This is a letter which I wish I never had to write to anyone . . . You have been a great friend, whose friendship is never-ending and true. You have looked well after me on the spiritual side. You have helped me be and made me a better person . . . so as the hour grows near I am trying to keep my faith, even in the face of what I must endure. I know I'm going to a better place with Jesus, but as a human it's hard to accept what's going to take place . . .
>
> With that, my very dear friend, I will say God bless you and good-bye until we meet again.

When Jim was executed along with another man, on March 22, 1997, Durlyn wrote, "Words cannot really express the feeling here [at the prison] after Wednesday's executions. Some guys still walk around in disbelief. It took me until Saturday to put myself together. Jim left this world very upset and I can understand that, he shouldn't have been put to death. . . . On top of all this, I received news Friday that my appeal in the District court was turned down. So now I'm one more step from being put to death myself."

In May of the previous year, Durlyn wrote me a letter shortly after the execution of John Wayne Gacy. Sister Miriam was among those who traveled to the prison to protest the Gacy execution. There were many others who arrived to cheer the event, and Durlyn expressed great concern for her safety:

> I know by now you are aware of the Gacy execution on Tuesday morning. It was a sad day for all involved in it. I have never seen anything like it before. It was, in fact, a circus with little kids and adults dressed up like clowns at midnight, singing, drunk and acting wild. They even harassed

the people who were there against the death penalty, which upset me.

A friend of mine was there along with Sister Miriam, who had just gotten out of the hospital. I had a feeling about the whole situation. I didn't want her to go but didn't say anything to her. But when I talked to her on the phone [later], I told her how I felt . . . thank the Lord none of them were hurt.

Another inmate, one whom I have known for some time, was transferred to Statesville Correctional Center shortly before Gacy's execution. In a note to me in the days after the execution, he wrote about the profound effect the experience of being close to this event had on him:

The execution of John Gacy brought out some very strong feelings in me. The day I arrived at Statesville, they were still housing Orientation inmates in X-House, where the execution would take place. So, the next morning, before being transferred to my assigned cell, I had the opportunity to see for myself the cell he would be detained in, the execution chamber, the witness viewing room and all the other preparations being made.

I remember wondering how I got in such a position where I would be standing in witness to such a thing. By the time the day of execution came, I knew why I had seen all these things. I was able to experience the emotion and empathy unadulterated. I wasn't afraid, but I experienced the death of him — and the hours leading up to it.

There was no judgment passed, however, I experienced some sadness at the loss of a human life. I found myself praying for him and the countless family members of his victims.

I could not help but think of Durlyn in the days after this execution. I continued to correspond with him and when Sister

Miriam passed away, he wrote to me again. "She will be dearly missed by all of us here. Sister Miriam brought a lot of hope to the men here, her joyful smile and kind words will forever remain with us. I know she is in peace now and she will always be in my prayers."

In our discussions and through his letters, Durlyn expressed remorse for the actions that brought him to death row. He viewed his misdeeds as aspects resulting from an illness he was unable to control. Although he accepted responsibility for his crimes and his incarceration, he did not believe he should have paid with his life.

"The court said I was a danger to society and to other inmates and I shouldn't be allowed to live," Durlyn wrote. Father Jonas Callahan, for many years the wonderful chaplain at Pontiac, had Baptized Durlyn during this time. When Durlyn conceded his fate he was more concerned with how others would be affected — particularly his friend, Eileen Bosshart, whom he had corresponded with for years.

"On November 11th, Eileen came to visit and we made plans for my burial. . . . So now I am preparing for my death." He wrote again just a few weeks later. "I'm at peace with myself and I was Baptized last Thursday. All the arrangements for my service are finished and invitations have been sent out."

Eileen was to hold a service at her home and Durlyn was concerned whether I would be able to attend. He wrote, " . . . maybe Patty can stop by and pick you up?" Imagine him worrying about my transportation to his funeral service just days before he was to die. "Sr. Josephine, this is our last letter, and when it comes to saying good-bye, I can't do it. . . . All the tears and the crying on the phone hurt me deeply. . . . I just want to say thank you for all that you have done for me — especially in opening up my mind and telling me about the Lord."

Eileen planned to visit Durlyn on the day of his execution, but the prison limited the number of visitors he could see. She did, however, speak to him that day, and later wrote to me describing his final hours:

The whole week before his execution was a nightmare for him. The prison with its rules caused him unbearable emotional suffering when they would not allow him his choice of visitors on his execution day. He spent needless frustration and anger trying to get changes made. I told him that Satan was using this means to deprive him of his peace of mind, and that he should spend his last hours free of anger or bitterness and close to Jesus in peace . . .

When he called me that morning from Statesville Prison, he sounded as "down" and discouraged as I had ever heard him. He could barely talk. He said he had stayed up all night and was so tired he could barely hold his head up. I learned from [his lawyer] that all throughout the morning as Durlyn tried to sleep, a guard came in to wake him up. Once the guard woke him up and complained that he was snoring too loudly . . .

Father Jonas Callahan told me that at the end he seemed to be at peace and free of any bitterness. I'm sure it was due to all the prayers that people were offering for him . . .

How good God is to listen to our every prayer, and even though Durlyn's life was not spared, he was the most ready for heaven at this particular time in his life than he has ever been in the past.

According to Father Callahan, Durlyn's last words were, "I love Jesus Christ my Lord." Eileen held a service for Durlyn at her home and, as mentioned previously, insisted that he be buried in her plot.

Durlyn had hoped that in some way the story of his life and death could someday, somehow be of help to others. Although he was estranged from many members of his family for years, he often talked of the everlasting bond that each of us finds in our mothers and fathers, sisters and brothers, daughters and sons.

In many letters to me, he seemed to express disappointment that in his life he was unable to truly appreciate the love of his family until it was too late. He stressed the importance that others learn from this mistake and understand that to take the love of family for granted is to ignore all that makes life worth living.

It's been 14 years, a very long time not knowing if I will live or die. My message to young and old is to come together as a family. Learn from and teach one another. A family is much stronger when you stand together. Love each other and sit down and talk out your problems with family ... You must hold the family together. That's all you have in this life besides the Lord.

Crucify Him! Crucify Him! Execute Him! Execute Him! These words would incite fear into the sturdiest of hearts. Was Jesus ever afraid? We have only to remember His words in the Garden of Gethsemane: "My Father, if it be possible, let this cup pass from me, not as I will, but as your will." (Matthew 26:30) The sinless Jesus knew that His opponents were coming to crucify Him. As He faced the prospect of bearing punishment for all the sinners of the world, Jesus Himself knew the darkness of fear.

These men on death row, acknowledging their guilt, have feared losing their life. They have made every effort to be spared because, like all of us, their thirst for life is ingrained in them. Nevertheless, they have made their own declaration, knowing that Jesus will not allow fear to overtake them, knowing that it is His will that will take them into heaven, and save them as He was saved.

The U.S. Supreme Court, in 1972, deemed the way in which capital punishment was being meted out as "cruel and unusual" punishment. It was not capital punishment itself that the court was critical of, but the arbitrary ways in which it was being applied. In 1976, urging states to proceed with caution and fairness, the court virtually reinstated capital punishment.

Since then, the death penalty has been viewed as a necessary measure to head off the rise in crime and violence in this country. Although statistics show that capital punishment has done little or nothing to reduce violent crime, Sister Josephine says it hasn't stopped some politicians from basing a career on this issue.

Time and again, these opportunistic politicians are backed up by polls showing that the majority of Americans support the death penalty. Most Americans, it seems, feel more secure in the knowledge that those who commit the most heinous of crimes are liable to pay with their life. Perhaps people see it as the only alternative for those whom we don't know what else to do with.

Pope John Paul II has expressed the church's stance against the death penalty, saying, "[Society] ought not go to the extreme of executing the offender . . . " However, the Pope continued by saying, " . . . except in cases of absolute necessity . . . when it would not be possible otherwise to defend society."

I don't believe there are any cases of absolute necessity when it comes to the execution of another human being. I don't believe that any real healing comes from the execution of another. I don't believe the death penalty serves as any true deterrent to violent crime and I don't believe God intends for any of us — as a person or a government — to possess the power of determining whether another person's life should be taken.

In addition, we as humans are imperfect beings. That means our judicial system is inherently imperfect — our judges, lawyers and jurors are imperfect. Wrongful convictions are not uncommon, even when it includes cases that seek the death penalty. We now know of at least 75 people who have been released from their cells on death row. A lethal injection cannot be reversed the way a verdict can.

In Jesus' life, He faced hate with love, evil with good. He was drawn to the most marginal members of society, outcasts like lepers, thieves and prostitutes. It was the marginalized that He preached to, the sick that He cared for and the powerless that He chose to inspire. Rather than punish, He chose to forgive.

As we strive to emulate the life of Jesus, everyday we are faced with our own human emotions — we feel pain, anger, frustration, confusion and even hate when our world is shaken by the assault or murder perpetrated by one on another. Locking the guilty party away may not seem like enough when a victim is scarred for life, or their life is abruptly and senselessly ended. Vengeance may seem the only path toward a justice that evens the score.

Antoinette Bosco, a columnist for the Catholic News Service, is the mother of a murder victim. In the March 1, 1996 issue of *The New World,* she expressed her human struggle with the death penalty in the wake of her loss:

> *I've heard all the arguments for the death penalty, and I don't dismiss them lightly. You can't arrive at opposition to this form of punishment with blinders on. When it hits you personally, the anger and pain of your loss make you want to tear apart the person who stole your loved one and your happiness. But does this do any good in the long run? And should we be in the business of killing people? Do we have that right?*
>
> *After my son and his wife were murdered in their home in Montana, I had to ask myself where I stood on the death penalty. It was one of the most intense moments of truth I ever struggled with. Strangely, I realized that I didn't want any more killing.*
>
> *I became overwhelmed with horror at the idea of unnatural death — murder of any kind, even when it is sanitized with labels such as "officials" and "lawful."*
>
> *The death penalty may be the most gut-wrenching moral dilemma of our time, precisely because the issue can't really be dealt with intellectually or even from our human perspective, but only through our higher selves.*
>
> *This issue is linked to faith, to God's territory — and that's the ground on which the debate belongs.*

In this country, what seems to have further legitimized the death penalty is the fear that if a prisoner guilty of a horrible crime is not put to death, he or she may someday be released to prey on society again.

Sister Helen Prejean, C.S.J., author of the best-selling book, *Dead Man Walking,* which was also made into a nationally acclaimed film, contends that the death penalty in this country is essentially reserved for the poor. Those with any wealth or those connected with anyone of prominence are less likely to be sentenced to die.

In the 1997 March/April issue of *Salt of the Earth,* Sister Helen wrote, "But when people of color are killed in the inner city, when homeless people are killed, when the 'nobodies' are killed, district attorneys do not seek to avenge their deaths." Besides, as Marie Deans, founder of Murder Victims' Families for Reconciliation (MVFR) has said, "An eye for an eye only makes the whole world blind."

No one in the fight against the death penalty intends to minimize the severity of any one's specific crime or the devastation it may have caused. The fight is with ourselves, to challenge ourselves with the question of whether we, in the name of the Gospel, are compelled to answer hate with hate, meet violence with violence or trade death for death. Jesus, after all, met His own enemies with compassion, mercy and love. You cannot change someone without love.

"A society is far down the road to decay when its religious leaders show as much tenderness to murderers and rapists as to their victims." So wrote columnist Jeff Jacoby in the *Boston Globe* after the late Cardinal Joseph Bernardin paid a visit to a man on death row. How could the Cardinal show such compassion to a murderer? this columnist wondered. A better question might be, how could he not show such compassion? An easy answer to each is: faith.

Our faith is challenged every time we face the human complexities of life. It is the strength of our faith that determines how we respond to those complexities. If we strongly believe that we are the children of God, a God of love and forgiveness, a God that asks that we forgive our brother not seven times, but seven times seventy times, then we ourselves are empowered and obliged to do as Jesus has done. For one who had dedicated his life to the service of the Lord, like Cardinal Bernardin, visiting a man sentenced to die is part of the job, and part of his faith.

Does the showing of concern for such a person have to mean the needs of their victims or their victims' family have been neglected? Does any compassion shown toward the sinner have to be regarded as an insult to those sinned against? Do the prayers offered up for the guilty have to be seen as a strike against the innocent? Or, in an effort to strongly separate right from wrong, to clearly distinguish good from bad, must we go beyond fear to hate, must we go beyond punishment to vengeance, must we go beyond prison to death?

Our faith is often tested in a way that pits the popular thing to do and the right thing to do. Cardinal Bernardin was certainly one unconcerned with what was popular. He was one who let God guide his path, his faith unshaken by what littered his way. For years he made a habit of celebrating Christmas Mass with the inmates of Cook County. Like Jesus, he was a forgiving friend to those in need.

When a young man who accused the Cardinal of sexual abuse eventually admitted deception, Cardinal Bernardin was the first to forgive. He met with the young man and they celebrated Mass together. In the book, *Bernardin: Life to the Full**, author Eugene Kennedy quotes Bernardin's Homily in that Mass.

> *In every family there are times when there is hurt, anger, or alienation. But we cannot run away from our family. We have only one family and so, after every falling out, we must make every effort to be reconciled. So, too, the Church is our spiritual family. Once we become a member, we may be hurt or become alienated, but it is still our family. Since there is no other, we must work at reconciliation . . .*

*Bonus Books, Inc.

When the Cardinal was diagnosed with pancreatic cancer and given less than a year to live, he acknowledged the humanness that serves as a constant test of our faith. Again, an excerpt from *Life to the Full:*

> *Nobody can be without fear and be human. And nobody can be without doubt either. But, as I've told many very ill people who worry about their fears and doubts, these go along with faith, they do not contradict it. That we have doubts does not mean that we do not have faith.*

It was the Cardinal's faith that not only compelled him to visit a man on death row, to forgive a man who accused him of a disgraceful act, and to reach out to so many others distraught with pain, but faith that calmed his human fear and doubt in the face of his own death. As Kennedy's book quotes him:

> *We can look at death as an enemy or a friend. If we see it as an enemy, death causes anxiety and fear. We tend to go into a state of denial. But if we see it as a friend, our attitude is truly different. As a person of faith, I see death as a friend, as the transition from earthly life to life eternal.*

When Cardinal Joseph Bernardin died November 14, 1996 — on his mother's 92nd birthday and the anniversary of his father's death — he demonstrated the ultimate power of faith. He was at peace in death because he knew peace in life.

Upon his death, I received heartfelt messages from many of the inmates, including one on death row, who wrote, " . . . I felt a deep loss [in learning of his death], and though I never met Cardinal Bernardin, deep in my heart I feel as if I've known him all my life." He went on to say that the Cardinal's courage and faith has left us inspired to "remember the many things he did to bring us all together . . . and to keep on moving for the better."

While death, as Cardinal Bernardin said, is "the transition from earthly life to life eternal," the calling to life eternal is one that should be left only in the hands of God. There are many who scour the Bible in search of quotes that might back up their belief in capital punishment. Biblical interpretation, as Sister Helen Prejean has said, can be a tricky business. "I cannot believe in a God who metes out hurt for hurt, pain for pain, torture for torture," Sister has written. "Nor do I believe that God invests human representatives with such power to torture and kill."

Sister Helen has capitalized on the recognition she gained through her best-selling book by continuing to speak out against capital punishment and providing a voice for the voiceless. She has also composed her views in a poetic prayer called, quite simply, "A Prayer to Abolish the Death Penalty."

God of Compassion,
You let your rain fall on the just and the unjust.
Expand and deepen our hearts
so that we may love as You love,
even those among us
who have caused the greatest pain by taking life.
For there is in our land a great cry for vengeance
as we fill up death rows and kill the killers
in the name of justice, in the name of peace.
Jesus, our brother,
you suffered execution at the hands of the state
but you did not let hatred overcome you.
Help us to reach out to victims of violence
so that our enduring love may help them heal.
Holy Spirit of God,
You strengthen us in the struggle for justice.
Help us to work tirelessly
for the abolition of state-sanctioned death
and to renew our society in its very heart
so that violence will be no more. Amen.

While inmates on death row have expressed their gratitude for those fighting to spare their lives, they are still confronted with the great possibility that the efforts of such people will not stop the state from eventually taking their lives. Each day they must wrestle with their fate, their faith and their ultimate destiny.

In reaching out to the Holy Spirit, some have been comforted by a new understanding of God's world, if not of the world around them. An inmate who now sits on death row has written to me about the mystical experience of feeling caught between these two worlds.

> To me, Paradise becomes a challenge. Have you ever felt like that? Wishing you could be there, yet be here at the same time to explain all of it to others?
>
> Some days I stretch out my arms and say, "God, take me home because I can't stand it here no more." Then, like a power of the Holy Spirit comes upon me and tells me, "Not yet, my son, you have not completed your journey there yet."
>
> . . . I sit here for hours wondering what will happen to me next. What great plan has God got for me? It is scary, Sister, the unknown of your destiny. Jesus knew His and followed each of His callings to the house of God in Paradise without reservation or fear.
>
> I want to be like Jesus, oh so very much. It gives me a sense of purpose and being, not like before when I didn't understand or care what it meant to know God and Jesus and the Holy Mother as I do today — the blessings, the miracles and gifts of peace and serenity, so calm and yet not ever alone . . . like I was before I knew God as I do today.

As Cardinal Bernardin said, "Nobody can be without fear and be human. And nobody can be without doubt either. . . . That we have doubts does not mean that we do not have faith."

7

Spiritual Awakening

Sister Josephine stands on an elevated platform in the recreation room of Division #8. On stage with her is a flimsy podium and a long, wooden table. The table is crowded with rosaries, paperback versions of the Bible, prayer cards and a bag of chewable candy. She pulls a few religious booklets from the bottom of her bag and adds them to the pile, but the squawk of an aging public address system is what holds her attention.

"A prayer service led by Sister Josephine will be held in the recreation room at 1:30 p.m. today. Any inmates willing to attend should register at the desk."

Sister Josephine shows a hint of a smile and then glances toward the back of the room, where two uniformed guards lean up against a pool table and a third lines up his next shot. "This ain't goin' down," one chides the man with the pool cue. "Watch it fall," he returns the volley before smacking the cue ball into another.

An inmate carrying a brown paper grocery bag emerges from a door at the back of the room which leads to the jail commissary — a sort of jail house convenient store. As he strolls past the pool playing guards, he reaches into the bag, pulls out a small package of potato chips and flips it into the ready hands of one of the guards. Keeping an eye on the scene, Sister Josephine shakes her head.

"We're just finishing up," one of the guards shouts to Sister. As the inmate continues out a door at the front of the room, a handful of others quietly parade past him and slide into one of several rows of wooden pews that are neatly aligned in the center of the room.

Continuing to prepare her display table, Sister Josephine reminds the assembling men that these religious materials have been bought with money donated to her. "Generous people use their money on you," she encourages them. "They think you are important enough that they contribute funds for your spiritual welfare."

The three uniformed guards scurry out of the room with their sticks in hand. "Pay attention now, not to me but to the Lord," Sister Josephine instructs her audience. A late arrival rushes into the room and, noticing his smirk, Sister Josephine says, "You're smiling, you must be converted." A few men chuckle.

At the prayer services, I am aware that each man who comes into that room is in need. Although they are all different ages, come from diverse cultures, have had distinct upbringings, are accused of varying degrees of crime, have had divergent exposure to religion and are in various stages of emotional upheaval, when they arrive at the services they have need in common. Their needs may vary as well, but it is need that has drawn each one of them there.

Through the services, I attempt to create an atmosphere that allows their needs to be met — even if one's need is to simply escape the strict routine of jail for one hour. That doesn't mean this time is to be treated as a social club. We conduct a service and, as I've said, those who are unable to respect the purpose of the service are asked to leave.

Most inmates attending a prayer service for the first time remain quiet, participating only in group prayer or song. Others have told me they are of another religious faith and prefer to observe the service and pray to themselves. Some are very depressed and say nothing despite attending week after week. Those cases, however, are rare.

The majority of inmates who continue attending the services eventually begin to participate enthusiastically. They begin to feel more comfortable and can no longer resist the natural temptation to open up. They free themselves from the force of their surroundings and their personalities gradually emerge.

Many inmates have written their own prayers, shared their stories with the congregation, performed solos at the service and helped distribute materials. Through the services, they seem to find some level of relief and, in turn, many discover the root of their need.

Tim told me he had no love in his life, that his search for love spurred a reckless cycle of women, wine and drugs. He once told me his incarceration was a blessing in disguise, and later wrote, "Going to a little prayer service in Cook County jail, of all places, was where I finally made peace with God and realized that my fate had been my choice, no one else's."

Tim was raised by his adoptive parents in a middle class home that promised all the hopes and dreams of a bright future. When his seemingly normal upbringing was shaken by the painful realities of life, he found himself vulnerable to the weaknesses that lie within all of us. I met Tim at one of the prayer services. He was handsome, intelligent and polite. In bits and pieces, I began to learn of his past.

> Looking at the picture next to my [prison] bunk, the picture with me and my first love in my convertible, I wonder where the time has gone. That one picture haunts my very being, that smile on that young boy's face. I'm not sure I know him anymore, for he was another person.
>
> Rewinding the thoughts over and over, I try and put together some sort of reasoning why my life didn't turn out exactly the way I imagined it would. Why was I the way I was? I guess, deep down, the only thing I ever wanted was a close family. But after the divorce of my parents, I soon discovered that was not going to happen. Maybe it was then I started compensating for the love I felt I never received at home. Somewhere through the turmoil of growing up, inse-

curity overwhelmed me and I never thought I was going to be good enough for anyone. To me, love was the only way I could feel whole . . .

Yes, going back to my past I can see where my feelings were in the way of reality. I wanted to live a dream-like life where no one left me and everyone was by my side. Fitting in then became what I desired the most. . . . I would trade anything for a night in a smoke-filled room with the light's turned low. But what I thought was a boy's night out turned out, year's later, as a fight to keep my soul, a fight that was nearly lost in the winds of time, slowly eating away at every single belief and piece of morality I had left. Drinking was a cure for all.

Tim's dream of being a photographer was lost to a lifestyle that revolved around drinking. Despite holding a job selling insurance, he continued to feed his bitterness and growing self-pity with self-destructive behavior. He says he blamed God for all that went wrong in his life and refused to take responsibility for his own actions.

On September 10, 1991, it all ended. The life that I loved to hate came to an abrupt end when I was arrested for committing my fourth armed robbery. It was also the last time I took a drink. This time, instead of spending the weekend drunk, I would be going through detox in jail. I had not missed a weekend of drinking for 10 years. . . . I didn't even know where I was until one of the girls I was dating told me when I called her collect [from the jail]. How could they have locked up a guy like me? I thought. I was no real criminal. But, I was.

During his time at Cook County jail, Tim went through many ups and downs. He was not yet equipped to confront his past and his problems, however, until he met the Lord. After attending many prayer services and a few private discussions, Tim came to me and asked if he could join the church. He told me his mother was Catholic but his father was not. When his parents divorced, he said his mother abandoned the church only to come back to the church when she was remarried. Tim was not sure if he had ever been Baptized, and no record could be found.

> ... the best place for me was that drug unit and finding out who God really was and how He was going to get me through this. . . . God has unleashed a new way for me to think and behave. He has done for me what I could never have done for myself. I now realize that God is my friend and He wants me to live the best way that I can: sober. Looking back through God's work, it was not the proud or the well-off people that He saved, but the meek and the poor. God has certainly given me a gift of great proportions that I must share whenever I can.

Tim was sentenced to 12 years in prison for his crime. Before he was sent to the penitentiary, however, he performed all the necessary work of preparing for his entrance into the Catholic faith. After due instruction, Tim was received into the church.

A February date was scheduled and Father Ted Ploplis, the chaplain of our hospital, agreed to administer the Sacraments of Baptism, Holy Eucharist and Confirmation. Tim looked forward to this day with great anticipation. I had secured all the necessary permissions needed for Father Ted to visit the jail. When we arrived at the jail, however, I learned that the superintendent I had spoken with had taken the day off. It was a holiday — Washington's Birthday I believe. I was told that I could enter the Division but that Father Ted could not.

It was getting late and Tim was waiting. I had the unfortunate task of telling him it was impossible to perform the Sacraments this day. Tim was very disappointed but I assured him we would return two days later. In preparation for our second attempt, I requested that his friends at the jail be given permission to witness his joy. Nothing doing. I was told by the officers that Tim, Father Ted and I were the only ones permitted to be involved in the service under such short notice. Despite another bureaucratic frustration, Tim was very happy to pronounce his faith that day.

When Tim was sent to serve his time in a penitentiary, he continued to find strength in his new relationship with God. He made the most of his incarceration by seeking positive activities and serving as a supportive friend to others.

> Since my incarceration I have done everything that I never imagined myself doing. I have gone to college and stuck with it. I received a degree in computer technology and have been accepted to a major university. God helped me do that. I take credit for nothing myself. It is a great paradox in life, when you give yourself to God you have more control over your life. . . . People forgive your wrongs not by how many times you apologize, but by your actions. Staying sober is the best way to show my family and friends just how much I have changed my outlook on life. . . . I have learned that God has everything He could possibly want except for one thing: our attention.

Tim was discharged from prison more than a year ago and has successfully completed his parole. With the help of the computer courses he completed in prison, he is now working for a computer company in Southern Illinois. He is newly married and has bought a home. I am very proud of Tim and my prayers are with him always.

Without warning, Sister Josephine begins singing "Amazing Grace" in a soft voice. She motions her recreation room parishioners to join in and helps by tossing out each verse before continuing in song. As the men respond, she adds hand-clapping, then feet-stomping, then hand-waving to various verses. Within minutes, the inmates have it down and like a polished church choir are belting out a theatrical version of the spiritual ballad.

As the song ends, Sister Josephine wonders if any of the men play guitar. "My cellie [cell mate] can play, Sister," answers a muscular, dark-haired man at the back of the room. Sister tells the men she keeps a guitar in a locker in another building but has been too busy to practice. "Maybe I'll bring it next week," she says excitedly. "So bring your cell mate."

As part of my ministry I have tried to make contact with the families and friends of as many inmates as possible. Throughout Tim's incarceration I was in contact with his mother. We exchanged many letters that dealt with the problems that led up to his arrest, how he would endure his sentence and how he would adjust to society once he was released.

Many times, inmates use their time in prison to reflect on their past, to analyze and begin to understand what went wrong, and to begin mending fractured relationships. In communicating with inmates and their family members, my hope is to help foster forgiveness and healing that can often be an overwhelming task for those involved.

I relayed to one inmate the letter his parents had sent me about their excitement over his pending release. I told him how lucky he was to have such a loving family that, with no questions asked, seemed ready to welcome him home with open arms. I joked with him that he was being received as a hero, so he'd better act like one. He is now married and doing very well.

So much of who a person becomes depends on the support one has received in the past. Many of the inmates I have come to know were raised in single-parent homes, in more than one foster home or group home, or by relatives who were compelled to take a child in. Many others are the product of what's been called dysfunctional families — in which neglect, abuse or a severe lack of attention and discipline are the norm.

Our society as a whole must bear some responsibility for failing to provide so many children with a solid support system, but the ultimate accountability lies with the adults in each child's life.

Each of us is called by God to acknowledge Him and, therefore, accept the meaning and purpose of our own lives. In Isaiah 6:8, to heed the cry of those in need, Christ asks us, "Whom shall I send?" And we answer, "Here I am! Send me!"

When I heard this reading at Mass not long ago, it occurred to me that we ought to apply these last lines as a prelude to each of the categories of people who affect the lives of children. Parents, can you say, "Here I am! Send me!"? Churches, can you say, "Here I am! Send me!"? Teachers and media, can you say, "Here I am! Send me!"?

Parenting should begin with marriage, which should begin with preparation. The vow of marriage is not one to take lightly, yet many enter into this lifetime commitment without laying the groundwork essential to a healthy relationship.

The first step toward marriage is the dating period, then engagement followed by marriage. It is truly wonderful when a man and woman meet, fall in love and plan a future together. The wedding begins their new life together. But engaged couples and those seriously considering it need time to focus on what a lifetime of marriage will mean to them — as individuals, as a couple, as a family.

With a divorce rate in this country that hovers close to fifty percent, adults planning to marry would be wise to take time for a reality check. Before they are married, partners should, at the very least, ask themselves and each other these basic questions concerning their future together.

What do you expect from marriage, from life? What are your goals? What are your attitudes on having and raising children? What are your attitudes regarding sex, religion, relationships with family and friends, careers and finances? How will you balance the demands of work, family and home? Are there essential qualities you couldn't stand to live with? Have family or friends advised rethinking your engagements? Have you considered these reservations carefully?

Look to God for strength. All discussion of marriage must recognize that God created marriage. Marriage is God's gift to us, but it is also a couple's gift to each other. Prayer helps others overcome trials and temptations. It centers life on God, the source of all joy, and acts as a reminder of His love and presence in all times, good and bad.

Marriage is not a short-term option, it is a contract for life ordered by God. The cornerstone and the foundation of a happy home is a spiritual exercise of prayer, Bible reading, and church attendance. Do you attend church? Do you read the Bible at home? Do you say a prayer asking for God's blessing at the table?

Pope John Paul II, in his *Letter to Families* (February 1994), wrote on the "profound truth of married life."

> ... *by describing himself to the bridegroom, Jesus reveals the essence of God, and confirms His immense love for mankind, but the choice for this image also throws light indirectly on the profound truth of married life. Indeed, by using this image in order to speak about God, Jesus shows to what extent the fatherhood and love of God are reflected in the love of a man and woman united in marriage.*
>
> *In the Old Testament and in particular in the Prophets, we find many beautiful expressions about the love of God. It is a gentle love, like that of a mother for her child, a tender love, like that of the bridegroom for his bride, but at the same time, an equally and intensely jealous love. It is not in the first place a love that chastises, but one which forgives, a love which comes to meet us just as the father does in the case of the prodigal son, a love which raises us up and gives us a share in the divine life. It is an amazing love, something entirely new and previously unknown to the whole pagan world.*

The church offers courses in the Cana and Pre-Cana programs. With the help of one or more married couples, a priest and sometimes a doctor, these programs have often been helpful in leading young women and men down the marital primrose path without being impaled by its thorns. Many times people wind up with a civil marriage without any preparation at all, but whether it is required or not, partners should do everything they can to ready themselves for this sacred lifetime commitment.

"The problem is not that kids are hungry or don't have shoes, or attend lousy schools," says writer and scholar Michael Schorr, "the emergency in this country, the issue that is affecting children the most, is the disappearance of marriage."

Time and again we read newspaper headlines where a young child is either the victim or the perpetrator of a violent crime. We instinctively wonder where their parents were. Everyone who enters into marriage must consider the fact that their life is altered once they are married, and altered again once they bear children. The most important ingredient in the life of your child is love. Are you prepared to love? If you are prepared to love, love will flow naturally from parent to child.

We cannot say I love God and others but I won't love me. Or, I love myself but have little regard for God and others. You are to love all three, God, self and others.

Every child is moved by the simple act of being touched by a parent. With your touch they are secure, they are loved. That love grows deeper and more powerful as you learn to love yourself and love God.

A favorite poem of Father Flanagan's Boys' Home reaches out to those blessed with the birth of parenthood.

Blessed Are the Parents

Blessed are the parents who refuse
to compare their children with others
Blessed are the fathers and mothers who have learned
to laugh for it is the music of the child's world
Blessed are those parents who accept
the awkwardness of their growing children, letting each child grow
*   at his own speed,*
Blessed are the parents who can say no
without anger,
Blessed are the parents who take their children
to church, for it gladdens their heart

Blessed are the parents who are teachable,
for understanding brings love
Blessed are the parents who love
their children in the midst of a hostile world,
for love is the greatest gift of all.

Parenting is a tough job, and it always has been. Couples enter marriage and have children, but many times are ignorant of what it entails to be a parent. It takes money, years of study, sacrifice and time to pursue most professions, but I have yet to see a course in parenting offered in college. But, there are signs of hope.

In Minnesota, parents now have the opportunity to participate in a 14-week parenting course at the same time and same place that their children receive child care. For those who can afford it, the cost is $85, but no parent is turned away. Those who cannot afford the course are asked to pay whatever amount they are able, and the state will cover the difference. This is a marvelous pioneer program that I hope and pray will spread to every state in the country, but I also hope that young men and women begin to learn about what it takes to be a parent long before they become one.

Being a good parent involves being willing to learn. Find out as much about parenting as you can and commit yourself to being an authentic role model. Parents who do not practice what they preach confuse their children. It is useless to ask children to be kind and generous, to avoid alcohol or drugs if their parents are mean-spirited, if they drink excessively or use so-called recreational drugs. Children need someone to look up to, models from whom they can learn to develop a strong sense of character.

This Dorothy Knowlton poem powerfully illustrates this point:

If children live with criticism,
they learn to condemn.
If children live with hostility,
they learn to fight.

If children live with shame,
they learn to feel guilty.
If children live with tolerance,
they learn to be patient.
If children live with encouragement,
they learn confidence.
If children live with praise,
they learn to appreciate.
If children live with fairness,
they learn justice.
If children live with security,
they learn to have faith.
If children live with approval,
they learn to like themselves.
If children live with an acceptance and friendship,
they learn to find love in the world.

As a parent, part of the job is to be in charge. This is particularly important in the teen years, when children are developing a sense of independence. First and foremost, talk to your children, do not be a stranger to them. Fight your reluctance to discuss delicate topics such as drugs, sex and violence.

Know your teen. Respect your teen's privacy but limit it. Be wary of what a teen keeps in his or her room. Be alert to what may be used as drug paraphernalia — matches, lighters, burned tin foil, cut up straws. Intervene when teens show signs of great change, such as sudden withdrawal from the family, slurred speech, disorientation, sudden decline in grades or new friends your child doesn't want you to meet.

What should you do if faced with the hard fact that your child may be using drugs? Don't panic and don't blame yourself. Resist guilt, shame or denial for it will serve no good purpose. At this time more than ever a teen needs to know you are going to stand by and love him or her despite bad choices. Confront your teen about this problem, but make sure the time is right for them to listen and understand. Finally, and most importantly, get professional help. A qualified counselor can determine the extent of your child's drug problem and help choose the right treatment.

"A Parents Prayer," by Christopher Metz, can serve as great inspiration when dealing with the most challenging job of parenting.

> *God our Father, You gave us life, Your life, and You enable us to give life to others. Watch over our children, Your children, protect them from the dangers of this day. Help them to know always that we love them, You love them.*
>
> *God our Father give us strength this day, help us to love with Your love, help us be an example for our children, to listen to them and to give them our time and energy. In the competing chaos of life, help us to know when our children need us, even when they don't say a word. Help us to answer with patience, wisdom and compassion.*
>
> *God our Father, remind us that You are always with us, holding us and our children gently in the palm of Your hand, cradling us in Your love and mercy. Amen.*

Those who are responsible for church parishes should say, "Send me!" Parishes can help foster effective communication techniques in a number of ways. In addition to sponsoring programs like retrouielle and marriage encounter, which usually take place over a weekend, churches can offer evening or one-day communication seminars. Experts from the local Catholic social service office or the Diocesan family life ministry could be invited to share their insights and advice. Of course, it helps if the pastor and other parish staff are familiar with the services that the local Catholic social services or other counseling agency has to offer.

Parishes can also sponsor youth groups — led by adults — which focus on religious education, character training, sports and entertainment.

Teachers can say, "Send me!" Most of us remember a teacher, youth minister or coach who encouraged us as a child, someone who looked at our efforts positively and took time not only to teach the curriculum but also instilled into our hearts and minds a sense of fair play, kindness and compassion.

I recently read about one such teacher, named Christopher Devink. One of his high school students, Michael, had difficulty doing school work and was repeatedly told that he was not college material, and was not likely to amount to anything. Devink encouraged Michael to develop his other talents. After graduation, Michael became a successful craftsman. He remembers his teacher as the one who gave him the incentive and confidence to take pride in his work and his life.

Today's young people are greatly influenced by television and the media in general. Media images tend to distort reality. The characters and lifestyles depicted in popular entertainment effect the way young people, especially teenagers, think and act. Violence, drugs and the abuse of sex are often glamorized. We get bombarded by the media's sensationalism of beautiful bodies, but finding someone to love and bond with is not all about model looks and sex. If we're buying what the media's saying, we'd better get over it or we're going to be terribly lost.

Parents, teachers and churches must counteract the media's distortions, to explain to children that television is not always applicable to real life, that it is an unreliable source from which to form an understanding of yourself and the world around you. Many mainstream television programs promote the notion that people don't need any commitments, that they are just free and young and wealthy forever. In fact, we're all vulnerable and in need of supportive relationships with family and friends. We need to connect with others for anything deep and profound to happen.

On the bright side, many colleges and universities are doing some very positive things for their students. They offer courses to young people that give real insight into Catholicism and other religious beliefs. In addition to providing them with an academic understanding of religion, however, many schools and universities are also getting students involved in community service activities. Thousands of college students either work or serve as volunteers in soup kitchens and shelters serving the homeless, in tutoring programs that serve the economically disadvantaged, in hospitals or agencies that help those suffering from AIDS, in day-care services or at nursing homes. Imagine what would happen in our cities if every college student were to take a confused teen under his or her care as a mentor.

While some college students spend their Spring Break on the beaches of Florida, others volunteer for organizations like Habitat for Humanity, which helps build homes for the poor. Other projects have included rebuilding Southern churches ravaged by arson. Through these school initiatives, students learn there is real opportunity to get involved. They also learn about the world around them, about their neighbors and about the great reward that comes from helping others.

We are all involved in parenting when we foster the healthy development of all children. Wendy M. Wright, an associate professor of theology and Coordinator of the Catholic Imagination Project at Creighton University sees parenting as a "charism." A "charism" refers to the specific work that defines a religious person or, their specialty. In the April 1998 issue of *U.S. Catholic,* she wrote:

> *I have come to see the spiritual gift of parenting as a distinctive form of love, which is itself the greatest of the charisms poured out by the spirit. I see it as a generative form of love: sent for the nurturing and raising up of the new generations . . . sent for the judicious preservation of past wisdom, the conservation of the soil out of which new life grows. It is a charism exercised by the mature, by mothers and fathers, so that the fullness of God's promises might continue to germinate in the body of Christ.*
>
> *I judge that the gratuitous charism of parenting may be bestowed on anyone within the Christian community who is called to do this essential, nurturing work. It might be discovered among religious educators, high school or grade school teachers, among bishops or members of sodalities, among spir-*

*itual directors or parish council presidents, among grand-
mothers or youth who parent those younger than themselves.*

*. . . At the same time I contend that the distilled experi-
ence of parental love is to be found and cultivated most explic-
itly among those who raise children.*

Wright goes on to say that she believes parenting to be the
greatest charism of them all. She lists a number of its specific
characteristics, including: making the children your first priority,
letting go of them by letting God offer care and protection as
well, being flexible enough to let your parenting grow with your
child and being able to find the common ground that enables
you to forgive, reconcile and heal your children.

Today our children are born in a "me-first" society. Family
life is said to be disintegrating, divorce is ever on the rise and too
many children are becoming latch-key kids. Many of these children are poor and lack the guidance of a father figure, but the
children of wealthy families fare no better when parents leave
them in the care of others day-after-day. These parents may
compensate their love and attention with material things —
from toys to cars — but these kids, once they are teenagers, can
also feel lost in a superficial world. Suicide rates among teens,
both wealthy and poor, remain alarmingly high.

These children should be preparing to become future parents, our country's leaders, exemplary Christians. Many of them
become statistics or inmates of our prisons. Who will rescue
them?

So many of the inmates I correspond with continue to express the repercussions of a painful or misunderstood childhood. "When I was 11 years old the State of Illinois took me
away from my family because I didn't attend school and I was
starting to get high . . . at the age of 16 I was returned home. I
was mad at my family for letting the state take me away. I had no
feeling for anyone so I wanted everyone I came in contact with to
feel the pain. . . ."

Scott Peck, the renown author of *The Road Less Traveled*, opens that book with a compelling quote, "Life is difficult. Once we accept it then life is no longer difficult." Later, he writes, "The quality of time parents devote to their children indicate to them the degree to which they are valued. When we love children they are a value to us, we spend time with them and enjoy their company. When parents are unself-disciplined they serve as poor models . . ."

In his *Letter to Families*, 1994, Pope John Paul II also addressed the vital role parents must play in the lives of our youth, and how that role changes as our children change.

> . . . *in every stage of his life, man desires to be his own person, to find love. During his youth he desires it even more strongly. The desire to be one's person, however, must not be understood as a license to do anything without exception. [Children] need guides and they want them close at hand. If they turn to authority figures they do so because they see in them a wealth of human warmth and a willingness to walk with them along the path they are following.*

Tough love can often be the most difficult part of the job for parents. Being both disciplined themselves, and able to discipline their children is often like balancing on a tight rope. Writer and humorist Erma Baumbeck may have put it best when she wrote, "I loved you enough to ignore what every other mother did or said . . . I loved you enough to allow you to stumble and fall, to hurt and fail . . . I loved you enough to say no when you hated me for it."

Many inmates have expressed to me the hope that they will learn from their past, from their mistakes and the mistakes of their parents. But as one inmate with a son awaiting his release put it, " . . . actions speak louder than words." He, and those like him, will return to a world that continues to change. The question they will face, however, remains the same. "Whom shall I send!"

8

Spreading the Good News

The men are standing now, each holding a sheet of music before them, their voices rising and falling together while the walls of the recreation room echo each verse.

With a wave of her hand, Sister Josephine brings silence to the room. "That was very nice, wasn't it?" she beams. The men return her smile and she asks for a volunteer to read a prayer.

A lanky man with dark glasses and worn canvas sneakers raises a hand and heads toward the podium. The reading revolves around suffering and as it ends, Sister Josephine prods the men assembled. "Do you find suffering easy?" she asks. "We have to accept bad things, don't we?" she answers herself. "But we all have to suffer for Christ."

Randy, the stocky brown-haired man who entered late, follows Sister Josephine's lead. He stands before the room and boldly tells of his family struggles and how he feels it relates to the suffering of Jesus. He wraps up his brief speech by saying, "Now I find real reason behind suffering, and I thank the Lord for it."

Others add their own testimonials to suffering and Sister Josephine moderates a discussion on how faith can help soothe pangs of depression and loneliness.

Kevin was a slight white male of about 30 years of age when I first met him at a prayer service. He always sat in the first row, paid strict attention, smiled constantly and asked pertinent questions. He also handed me a letter one day before leaving the service.

> Sister, I anticipated that our time would be rushed and brief as is often the case on Thursdays, and that is why I have written you this note. I hope that sometime in the future we have a chance to sit and chat, though I have that suspicion my expectation is a bit too optimistic. As you told me a few weeks ago, you would like to have time for a chat as well. I'm not sure whether you have the freedom in terms of time to do this, but I'd like to suggest we try to correspond through the mail. Perhaps that's the best way for questions to be asked and answered considering the circumstances.
>
> After writing that, I'm not quite sure how to continue. My past has had many ups and downs, filled with constant walks to and away from God . . . which is fairly common for most people. I have felt that "special purpose" which you saw in me the first day we met, though I can't quite seem to get completely in touch with it. Maybe now is the time.
>
> While I am not a Catholic, I have felt drawn to the church often during the past twelve to thirteen years. What I am experiencing now is the deepest expression and profession of that. I'm finding such a good avenue of experiencing the Christian faith through the Catholicism I see, and I sense an urge or need to be a part of that. Even in terms of something like the rosary, which I don't know but want to learn, I'm finding desire in what has not been a part of my upbringing . . .

The following week I told Kevin I try to make time to talk with anyone who would like to, that it wasn't necessary to correspond by letter at this time. After that, we did meet many times to "chat" at Cook County jail, but before long Kevin was sent to a penitentiary in Southern Illinois. That's when our letter writing began. We have corresponded for the past 11 years. Kevin has come a long way in that time. Like Tim, he demonstrated a genuine interest in looking to God for help in changing his life.

Kevin impressed me from the start. He's a born leader, intelligent, caring and loving. As he gradually became more acquainted with the spiritual life, he came to love and appreciate the Lord and just couldn't get enough religious reading.

> I'm slowly reading a super book by Thomas Merton, *No Man Is An Island*. It was given to me by a retired Protestant pastor. Merton sure is challenging! I can see why many felt threatened by him, as many felt — and still feel — threatened by Jesus.
>
> I have enclosed a booklet which I hope you will enjoy. With our shared love and respect for Our Lady, I know you will like it. And I want to thank you for the article you sent regarding the ordination of older men.
>
> You know me well . . . maybe better than I do myself. And, by the way, I hope you know that you are partly to blame for me being "so widely read in things of the Lord" as you claim I am! I wish I retained a bit more and I'm sorry photographic memory is not a gift Christ thought I needed. This old collection of melted down brain cells will have to do — the Holy Spirit has His work cut out for Him, and the many good things you have given me to read have definitely exercised my brain and my spirit. So it's your fault. (Smile!)

Besides having the time to read, Kevin also liked the sense of community in the jail. He was always looking to help someone in need. He once learned sign language in order to help a deaf inmate understand what was happening at their substance abuse meetings, and he often referred me to inmates who might use my help or attention. He also took education courses. In one of his English classes, he was assigned to write a character sketch on someone he had come to know.

> She is barely five feet tall, yet Sister Josephine Migliore, M.S.C., possesses within her the strength, compassion,

feistiness, persistence, and love of more than a dozen souls. Even if someone wanted to forget her, it would be an impossible project. But only a fool or the coldest of hearts would try.

It's kind of funny — the Bible mentions those who storm the gates of heaven, taking/obtaining the Kingdom of God as if by force, and the sweet, tiny figure of Sister Josephine might very well fit that bill. Without seeing her in action, it's probably hard to imagine, though you witnessed her take on jail guards, officers, and other powers that be, with an unabashed forthrightness which would challenge the toughest marine. No mountain is too high or wall impenetrable enough to dissuade her.

However, she is not some ruthless crusader. As a matter of fact, Sister Josephine is probably the kindest and most merciful person to sit down and listen to, reach out to, and accept a person in need, whether it's on a temporal level or a spiritual one.

I never met Mother Theresa of Calcutta, Therese of Lisieux, Mother Cabrini, or any of the other recognized "saints" or saints-to-be, but from what I've read about them and of their own writings I find a unique synthesis of them in Sister Josephine. She radiates Christ: the one who without zealous cleansed the Temple and the one who, in love and boldness, healed and associated with society's outcasts. Yes, Sister Josephine is very unforgettable — and I'm positive neither God nor I would have it any other way.

It was not long before Kevin was sure he wanted to become a Catholic. Along with the Kocars, a couple that was part of the ministry team at the time, I worked with Kevin in preparation for studying the faith. He too was accepted into the church.

As in the case of Tim, our request to administer and celebrate the Sacraments to Kevin with all the inmates at a prayer service was not granted. Instead, with me serving as his sponsor and his friend as a witness, our ministry team performed the ceremony. Kevin was Baptized on November 3rd of that year.

As quiet as his Baptism was, Kevin's Confirmation was attended by almost all the inmates of Division #8. The late Cardinal Joseph Bernardin made a routine of saying Christmas Mass at the jail. In 1988, he was scheduled to celebrate Mass in Division #8. The Cardinal graciously administered Confirmation to Kevin during that Mass. It was a wonderful day.

> . . . I'm so happy and blessed that you were here to share what will always be a uniquely special day and moment. You have been with me to help me through my journey of faith at especially important points. From my catechism to Baptism and now on to Confirmation at the hands of one of God's most trusted servants . . . you have been by my side. I just cannot tell you how much it all means to me. As unworthy as I am Christ has made it quite clear that He wants me and has surrounded me with grace upon grace . . .
>
> Wasn't Cardinal Bernardin great?! He was so impressive yet it wasn't in some grand and spectacular fashion. As you and others have told me, the grace he emanates really comes through in his warm and friendly simplicity. I have yet to wash my right hand and forehead, and I wish I could bronze both. But I can't stay on the mountain top forever and there's a distinct advantage in being clean! Oh well, I'm sure I'll wash up at least once before your next visit (smile!).

While I knew Kevin's spiritual awakening was of great help in cleansing the sins of his past and offering hope for his future, I was not sure how he would withstand such a long prison sentence.

> You asked if I thought I would survive these past ten years. It's funny you should ask, especially as I recently passed the tenth anniversary of my arrest and imprisonment. Early on I don't think I had any concept of what awaited me. Then, shortly after actually coming to prison I really doubted I would make it. I was tempted by suicide,

scared by gangs, and forced to face what I had done . . . something I had buried fairly deep. As you may remember, I went through a type of nervous breakdown. Thank God I survived in spite of myself and, with a great deal of grace and patient support, I think I have emerged stronger, wiser and more mature.

Certainly I've come away OLDER. Yet I've also learned, as you wrote, that "all is possible with God." As to whether or not I'll be able to see [my son] again, I'll simply have to wait and see.

You asked how much longer I have in prison and it's actually not too long to go until I'm out. As of now I'm due out in January of 1998. However, this month I'm applying for an extra 90 days of "good time" which, if I receive it would put me out in October of next year. Whether I receive the good time credit or not is a matter of prayer and speculation yet, one way or another, there is definitely a lot of light at the end of the tunnel nowadays!

In the many letters I have received from Kevin over the years, he has always maintained his unique sense of humor. With his faith in God, I think his ability to laugh, and make others laugh, has really helped him survive. When I told him I had been asked to make a presentation at a meeting, he responded in just the way I expected.

. . . Am I reading this correctly, you were asked to get on stage and perform at the meeting of Associate Membership?! I wish I could have been there to cheer you on. It's funny that you mentioned your stardom, because just the other evening I watched the movie, "The Singing Nun" (starring Debbie Reynolds). Perhaps you should consider doing more with this new facet of your vocation! Think of it: TV appearances, recording contracts, albums, etc. And who knows, when they make a movie of your life maybe Debbie Reynolds can play the lead role!!

Close to eight years ago Kevin ended one of his letters imagining the day when he could look back on many years of partnership with the Lord.

> If the way you bounce around and plow ahead now is any indication of what 76 years with the Lord is like, I can't wait to catch up with you! And, even though it's not exactly Scriptural, since paradise isn't measured by time, I may just catch up to you one of these days . . . so you had better be ready! Gee, I hope I'm ready!! (smile).

Kevin was released in January of 1998 after serving more than 10 years in prison. He begins a new chapter of his life as, in many ways, a new man. He can already look back on a long and healthy relationship with God. But is he ready to continue nurturing this spiritual commitment outside of the confines he's known for so long? Only he can answer that, and I believe he has.

In an essay he wrote about his experiences and his transformation, he seems to articulate the feelings of many who find themselves not only imprisoned from society, but imprisoned from themselves and their own physical and spiritual existence.

> Christ is a whisper away from Hell: I know that to be true after having been incarcerated since 1986. During my only "bit" in jail or prison, Christ has heard the whispers of this exile and He has spoken to me through many special people. By doing so, He has proven to be closer to me than I had once believed.
>
> Inmates are encouraged to develop a devaluation of the people around them while incarcerated. As I did, many of them bring at least some of the necessary attitudes and behaviors with them as they enter the system — where they become finely tuned in exile.
>
> Dishonesty, anger, racism, aggression, disobedience, paranoia, cruelty, and coldness become the prized survival skills against the ever-present fear, loneliness, ignorance, and doubt encountered during imprisonment. The first

dogma of jail house philosophy says it all: "Kindness is Weakness." Coupled with other gems like "Fight the Power" and "Trust No One" (Principles of "life" reinforced by an inmate's own failures, flaws in the criminal justice system, and the disappearing acts or distancing offered by some spouses, lovers, friends, etc.). It is no wonder why inmates disregard the consequences of such thinking. Nor is it surprising to see those values and resulting actions returning to society upon an inmate's release. However, I have also seen and experienced Christ's response to the cult of devaluation just this side of Hell. He offers true worth.

Jesus Himself has proven to be a whisper away from Hell by using the people in my immediate field of vision. In the midst of a neighborhood of potential enemies, Christ has faithfully listened and spoken to me through the believers He has raised up among my fellow inmates. There have always been men of God near me in jail and prison. They have either been newly converted, recently put back into a right relationship with Christ, or wrongly imprisoned. Among the many others I have met over the years, Christian inmates like Fred, Raphael, Scott, Tom, Angel, and Miguel have stood for Jesus and against fear. They have actuated the very first verse of Sacred Scripture I heard during my initial night in jail: "The Spirit God has given us is no cowardly Spirit, but rather one that makes us strong, loving, and wise" (2 Timothy 1.7).

The Lord has also been consistently present through Christians specifically involved in jail and prison ministries. I continue to be amazed, challenged and strengthened by their faithfulness to Christ and to supporting my walk with Him. Too few inmates or segments of society are touched by people with such faith and commitment. Sister Josephine, Marv, Peg, Harry, Richard, Jay, Russell, Deb and others like them have helped to transform my loneliness and misdirection. Through them Christ honors an important promise first made to His early disciples: to always be with His people and never leave them orphaned (cf. John 14.16–18).

I have been further blessed by the Lord with excellent teachers while incarcerated. Since my imprisonment, I have seen much of the extravagant ignorance which is not simply allowed, it is actually fostered in jail and prison. As citizens and politicians voice real concerns regarding crime, current efforts to cut educational programs in prison only fuel the detrimental blaze of misconceptions relative to fighting crime, as well as sin. In addition to wise spiritual teachers, Christ has always been nearby in Marcia, Dan, Jay, Ann, Mike, Don, Laurie, and other excellent instructors of career skills and formal education. Though they may soon be prevented from sharing their God-given gifts with inmates, I have been blessed by the many ways they have helped replace ignorance with knowledge. And while Christ may have meant it solely in regards to spiritual education, the fact that truth does set people free (cf. John 8.32) has been confirmed for me by many teachers in other subjects during my exile.

In the face of doubt, Jesus has provided me reassurance in terms of family. Even though I cannot imagine how the blessings I have received could be worth the cost — to Christ or to those who have had to suffer because of my past actions — the Lord has used this experience to help me truly appreciate and love my family. My parents have become the wisest and most interesting people I have known. After years of my trying to manipulate or avoid them, Jesus has shown me that I have never been a product of bad parents. My brother is as loyal, hard-working, talented, and humorous as anyone in my life. Unfortunately, it took imprisonment and God's grace for me to finally realize that fact and to value my three best friends.

Moreover, no one could have desired a better wife or son than God once gave me, yet I wrongly mistook their worth to me. It is only thanks to God's mercy that I will ever see them again, or the former in-laws who also deserved a far better person than I was before my exile in 1986.

Christ's familial reassurance has further broadened beyond merit or expectation. Jesus has introduced me to a family of saints previously unappreciated by me — saints who encountered obstacles far worse than mine — exemplifying real faith in doing so. While in prison I've become acquainted with such members of His family (and now, of mine) as Abraham, Ruth, David, Mary, Peter, Augustine, Francis, Ignatius, Theresa, Frances, Maximillian, Dietrich, Martin, Thomas, and numerous others. The reassurance I continue to receive through the renewing of one family and my spiritual connection to another is proof to me of God's power and desire to offer families as a sign of Christ's forgiveness, love, kinship, and nearness (cf. Luke 15.32; Ephesians 5.22–33; Mark 3.35; Malachi 3.24).

In spite of being at a doorway to Hell, I have discovered Christ listening and speaking to me during my incarceration much as God did to an earlier collection of exiles:

> *"The Lord, your God, is in your midst, a mighty savior; He will rejoice over you with gladness, and renew you in His love, He will sing joyfully because of you, as one sings at festivals.*
>
> *I will remove disaster from among you so that none may recount your disgrace. . . . I will save the lame, and assemble the outcasts. . . . At that time I will bring you home, and at that time I will gather you. . . . when I bring about your restoration before your very eyes, says the Lord." (Zephaniah 3.17–20)*

The original exiles of which the above verses speak found in their incarceration the same God I have come to know during my legal exile. His presence and voice are always near, even a whisper away from Hell.

The ultimate gift of this ministry for me has been the opportunity to not only share my great love for God, but to make God known to those who have shut Him out of their lives. The prayer services have proven the most effective and, perhaps, the most unobtrusive way to open inmates up to the word of the Lord.

My hope is that once they begin to realize that God holds the key to turning their lives around, they will be quick to share their faith with others in need. I am delighted to say that inmates like Kevin have served the Lord well in continuing to carry His message to those they encounter in the jail and in penitentiaries across the country. One inmate has kept me updated on his continual work with a mutual friend.

> Sister, as God inspired you to use tough love with Bill, he openly shared your letter with me and he was willing to admit a little possibility that if you and I both were telling him growth is necessary in life then he would consider thinking about it.
>
> . . . He talks about his conviction to me, but continues to deny any responsibility. We know God loves Bill and continues to shower him with opportunities for growth.

Another inmate has made it his mission to speak to the younger men of his prison. Although he did not attend the prayer services when he was being held at Cook County, he has since found a reason to let God into his life. He tells me he relies on his own experiences to show others another way. "It's time for them to wake up and get God in their lives. I let them know I may never be leaving this place, and if they don't leave this kind of life behind them they will be here like me," he has written. "Most of them don't want to hear it, but if I can make one of them think twice, then I feel great."

Over the years, this kind of outreach has virtually transformed my ministry from a weekly, on-site approach to an almost mail order variety. With so many inmates in so many places requesting religious materials — from books and bibles to rosaries and prayer cards — I have been blessed with the challenge of keeping up with all of the postage and paper work.

There have been countless times when I have received a letter from an inmate requesting a book that he thinks would be an encouraging read for a friend. Others read one book by a specific author and immediately write me requesting anything else by the same author — send me more DeMello, Aquinas, Nouwen. I have given away more copies of *The Peace Pilgrim* than I could ever care to count. One inmate wrote me to tell me how moved he was by that book, and how much he wished he were able to meet her.

Like the loaves and the fishes, the Gospel continues to feed more and more hungry people simply through the introduction of God. "To have a spiritual outlet in prison means a great deal for those who believe in the Lord or are seeking to learn more about him," read one inmate's letter. "I have attended Sunday Mass here at Centralia for the last two weeks. I remember being in Bible study where the preacher stated how easily we take our focus and faith off the Lord and suddenly put our faith in a lawyer. I found that to be a most interesting point."

Another wrote, "As long as I have God in my life, nothing can go wrong. I have so many things I want to do once I get on my feet, but the most important thing I want to do is get together with you so I can make my first Communion and start going to church on a weekly basis . . . "

One inmate, who was not Catholic, continued to ask me if I would give him a rosary. I was wary of inmates who might use a rosary to make some sort of gang symbol. This man told me he had nightmares every night and hoped a rosary could help them go away. I finally gave in to him. When I saw him a few weeks later he told me that when he wore the rosary around his neck at night, he had no nightmares. When he didn't, he said they returned.

Another inmate wrote, " . . . Now that I've lived for the Lord I am at peace . . . I just thank Him for every new day He gives me, in the hopes that I can pass His word onto someone else who may need Him."

To accept God's love is not to be consumed by it, but to share it. Those who have discovered the Lord have also discovered themselves, others and a whole new world. One inmate seemed almost awestruck in the changes he experienced after opening up to God's love:

> ... Wanting to change my life I decided to go to church one day and that's where I met you .... I have in six short months obtained my high school diploma, am working on a college degree, have found a church that teaches the truth, and am looking forward to the day that I am officially accepted into it, for that I thank you. You have truly helped to change my life ...

I have been greatly enriched by the people and the process of this ministry and am comforted in knowing that many inmates will continue this work when I am unable.

I am also hopeful that society as a whole will work toward a change in attitude regarding the function of the prison system in this country. The "lock them up and throw away the key" approach has only caused more division, more recidivism and more prisons. In following this path, we risk separating our society into two primary communities — those on the inside and those on the outside.

The prison population in this country is close to 1.7 million inmates, and that number is projected to reach 2 million by the year 2000. Russia is the only country that exceeds the U.S. in the number of citizens it has incarcerated. The annual cost of an inmate is said to be anywhere between $20,000 to $70,000 per year.

We cannot continue to spend millions and millions of dollars building prison after prison across this country. We can try, but ultimately we will be confronted with the hard truth that locking people out of society may be as damaging to ourselves as it is to them.

The issue certainly is complex, but in a society founded on the principles of "equal opportunity," it seems that a natural extension of that opportunity should be afforded to those detained in prison as well. Inmates who have taken advantage of the opportunities offered — academic courses, substance abuse programs, group therapy and religious services — have demonstrated a will to change.

Through activities that promote not only self-worth but self-esteem and personal responsibility, many inmates have for the first time felt a sense of purpose and meaning in their lives. It is only natural to think that by equipping them with the knowledge, skills and confidence to contribute to society, their chances of avoiding the pitfalls of their past once they are released are greatly minimized.

In a sign of hope for more positive changes in the prison system, last year the first military-style boot camp in Cook County was established. Offenders between the ages of 17 and 35 who have never committed a violent or sex-related crime and who have not served more than a year in a state prison are given the choice to serve time in jail or participate in this alternative program.

The program encompasses 18 weeks of intensive, military-style training and, perhaps more importantly, an 8-1/2 month supervised post-release program. In addition to the officers, the staff includes teachers, counselors and psychologists. The inmates are offered educational and vocational training and are given responsibilities such as cleaning their own sleeping areas and doing their own laundry. While the men are given recreational privileges, there is no television. The only reading materials permitted are textbooks and the Bible.

This kind of program, which mixes discipline with opportunity, may serve as an example that inmates can turn their lives around when given the proper tools and necessary support.

It is understandable to question whether those who commit crimes against society should be rewarded in prison with opportunities that they either ignored or were unable to attain outside of prison. To me, this is a philosophy of not only piling punishment on top of punishment, but of denying some the chance of redemption, rehabilitation and recovery.

It seems only sensible, especially in the case of inmates who will one day return to society, that they be afforded the opportunity to return to society a better person. Close to 20,000 people are released from Illinois prisons each year, but if punishment is all that is offered in prison, chances are a good majority of these people will return to the streets only more equipped to succeed in a criminal trade. When discipline is mixed with group and private counseling, skill-building courses and the freedom of religious practice, inmates are exposed to another way of thinking, another way of behaving and another way of living.

This same approach can be carried over upon an inmate's release so that transitional programs will be better able to help an inmate succeed on the outside. This is already being done on a small scale. Many organizations, including St. Leonard's House and Grace House of Chicago and Catholic Charities' sites nationwide, continue to work with inmates in adjusting to their new life. Not only do organizations like these offer temporary housing and work with released convicts in finding employment, they offer therapeutic counseling, employment-training programs and parenting- and anger-management workshops. In specific cases, they require participation in Alcoholics Anonymous or Narcotics Anonymous. In setting expectations for these men and women, they are raising the expectations of their recently released clients.

But leaders of these organizations say that due to a lack of resources and companion programs, they are only capable of admitting a fraction of ex-offenders. If society is to hold optimistic expectations for the majority of released convicts, more programs like these must be implemented and provided with the necessary, long-term support they need to survive and succeed. In the same way that businesses are encouraged to become emotionally and financially supportive of programs working with disadvantaged youth, they should also offer this attention to programs that strive to turn convicted criminals into productive, self-sufficient citizens.

Ultimately, the men and women of these programs must take personal responsibility, they must hold up their end of the bargain and make a profound commitment to change. It is doubtful, however, that they can do it alone. Without a solid support system and an inspiring attitude of change, more and more inmates will find themselves relying on desperate measures of survival — which means they will continue to pose a threat to society.

At the same time, this approach should be complemented with a renewed focus on prevention. Many of the inmates I have come in contact with have admitted being aware of their destructive path long before they were arrested. While some ignored offers of help, others have told me they did not know where to turn for help. More programs and stronger outreach is just part of the answer. It seems to me a change in cultural attitude will hold the key to whether our prison population will continue to rise to exorbitant levels.

Today, there are some encouraging trends working to counteract the many negative aspects of society. A change in climate can be seen in national organizations such as the Promise Keepers. Last year, close to one million men gathered in Washington, D.C. in a communal promise to uphold their responsibilities to their families and neighbors. They asked pardon of their spouses, children and especially of God for neglecting their families in the past and prayed for the strength to overcome their weaknesses and rely on their faith.

Some women in the country criticized this group, complaining that women should have been invited as well. While I understand their grumbling, I do believe men of this country share many common responsibilities. As a group they felt they had let their families down and wanted to publicly acknowledge their sins and pronounce their renewed commitment.

Inspired by the Million Man March, thousands of African-American women gathered in Philadelphia last summer to share, reflect and re-energize the responsibilities they have carried for many years. Perhaps one day these groups can gather together, but these events serve as a reminder that in this increasingly hi-tech age we must maintain our sense of community.

I recently learned of a National Summit of Fatherhood, headed by the governors of Eastern states, which promotes family life legislation. Also, there is a National Evangelical Team in which young people dedicate a period of their lives to evangelize.

In 1993, I attended the World Conference for Youth in Denver. Pope John Paul II was received by the young people there with the chant, "Holy Father, we love you!" He answered, "Holy Father loves you, too." This went back and forth and eventually the Pope said, "The Holy Father loves you more . . . "

There is a program on EWTN television network called "Life on the Rock." It is an upbeat but solid teaching of the church and its activities presented by youth primarily for youth. It's very heartening to see young people give their testimony to having been converted to good living, drug-free lives, and lives of meaning to themselves and society.

In the church there is the Eucharistic Adoration in many cities. For a time, Benediction of the Blessed Sacrament seemed to be passé, and people didn't care to go anymore. I believe that's why the church experienced a decrease in fervor and attendance, but now many parishes have 24-hour adoration, and the best part is that it has been initiated and overseen by the laity.

Leaders of the parishes stepped forward and in many parts of the country Our Lord is being exposed through the Blessed Sacrament and people pray, not only during the day but all night long at a great sacrifice because many of them have to work. Some are parents who take care of kids during the day and in the evening give one full hour or more of telling Jesus how much they love Him and want Him to be a part of their lives and the lives of those they love.

It is my hope that more and more of these encouraging trends will seep into our society, which includes our brothers and sisters of the prison community.

In a culture where many people replace the love of God with the desire for drugs and alcohol, we may find that the search for treatment lies within each one of us.

9

The Power of Transformation

The service continues with prayer, discussion and song. Finally, noting the time and the sticky heat that's filled the room, Sister asks if anyone else has something to add before ending today's service.

A crew-cutted inmate rises to his feet. "I quit going to church years ago, Sister," he begins, "but I think I've been praying for you. My cell mate told me about you Sister and this is my first time here. But since I just got sentenced to 20 years, this is also my last time here. I will be moved to a penitentiary tomorrow."

The pale-faced man glances down at the floor, then around the room before focusing again on Sister Josephine. "I'm glad I came here today and I'm glad you will still be here for my brothers," he says in a quivering voice. "I know what I have to face now. It doesn't matter where you find yourself. You put my mind at ease, Sister, and I love you for that."

The congregation erupts in applause. As the crew-cutted young man sits down, an older man seated to his left offers a consoling pat on the back. "Thank you and God bless you," says Sister Josephine before instructing him to see her after the service. "Now let us pray for you."

The room grows silent and Sister begins to pray aloud for the courage this man has shown in sharing his feelings. The crew-cutted inmate, she learns later, was convicted for murdering a friend

*while under the influence of drugs. As she continues in prayer —
asking God to grant this man both forgiveness and strength — one
inmate in the group can be heard reciting the "Our Father" in a soft
tone.*

Sometimes I wonder how many of the men and women
now serving time in prison would never have seen the inside of a
jail cell if our society were not overrun by drug and alcohol
abuse. Ironically, many admitted addicts say that being arrested
and incarcerated may have saved their lives.

The introduction of substance abuse programs to the
prison population may be the most encouraging development
our judicial system has seen in decades. The Gateway Substance
Abuse Program was introduced to Cook County jail in 1968 and
is still meeting the needs of so many inmates.

Although not every inmate of every jail or prison is afforded this opportunity, a great number of them have been accepted or directed to such programs. These programs vary in size
and scope, but they are all designed to help these men and
women overcome their illness.

Most of the programs found inside and outside of prison
are based on the principles of Alcoholics Anonymous (AA),
whose principles are rooted in medical and religious concepts.
AA was founded in 1935 in Akron, Ohio by two men suffering
from alcoholism. In taking the alcoholic's point of view, these
men set out to prove that alcoholism could be tempered and developed AA's Twelve Steps toward recovery. The AA concept is
known and shared internationally and the organization is said to
have a membership of more than one-hundred thousand.

One of the inmates gave me a book published by Alcoholics
Anonymous called *Twelve Steps, Twelve Traditions,* and inscribed
it by saying he wanted me to know what he would "try to live by
each day." This book lays out each step in great detail and also includes case histories that outline the destructive path down and
the constructive path up.

The 12 steps are filled with references to God and AA's unofficial code is the Serenity Prayer: "God grant me the serenity to accept the things I cannot change, the courage to change the things I can, and the wisdom to know the difference." The AA model is simple but successful.

Studies have shown that people who experience a great deal of trauma or stress in their lives are more likely to become addicted to drugs. Those who are surrounded by drug users, experts say, are also more susceptible to develop addictions. This tends to breed what is often referred to as a "drug culture," where friends encourage and persuade each other to continue their habits.

The capitalistic pursuits of America, some people believe, in many ways continue to feed the drug epidemic. In a society where success is often measured in terms of wealth, possessions and image, some say drugs serve as an alternative to those who feel they don't measure up. Others say that drug dealing and drug using offer the disenfranchised the chance to be good at something. Drugs, they maintain, offer the dispossessed some purpose in their lives.

Although inmates say it is possible to obtain drugs in prison, they are reminded everyday where their reliance on drugs or alcohol has landed them. In my experience with those participating in the Gateway program of Cook County jail, I have witnessed many personal transformations — in thought, behavior and hope.

"Going to the drug unit was the best thing that ever happened to me," one inmate relayed to me not long after being accepted into the Gateway program. "I now see that I allowed drugs to rule my life. It's time for me to learn how to be in control."

This former gang member, drug addict and husband continues to write to me about his past and his progress. He says he now sees glimpses of his former self in the many new arrivals to his prison wing.

I've come close to death many times. Some of the guys I grew up with were not so lucky. I guess it's true that the Lord works in strange and mysterious ways. My being sent to prison, I must admit, is a blessing. The bottom line is I was killing myself. . . . As you probably are aware, the great majority of new inmates coming into the system are coming in for drug-related offenses. For many it's an Act of God, their lives were totally out of control. Many inmates express the feeling that despite the negative experience of being incarcerated, that they were in the long run saved from self-destruction. Unfortunately, many of these new inmates have very long sentences to do. By the time they are free again, it is pretty sure that their whole family life will have changed.

Because many alcoholics and drug addicts, as it is said, are the product of a parent or other close relative who suffered from addiction, this illness is often carried on from generation to generation.

Whether this is a physical or environmental transfer, it is safe to say our society has proven a demanding marketplace for such products — both legal and illegal. The consequence is an ever-widening demand for programs that help people battle their addictions. But that doesn't mean that the demand for alcohol and drugs has shown any sign of decreasing.

Today, many children who grow up in impoverished communities see drugs as a part of their culture. In many neighborhoods where unemployment is high and expectations are low, the sale of drugs may be seen as one of the few sources of income. Although parents may try to shield them from the realities — if they are not a part of the drug industry themselves — children are quick to observe that drug dealers are seen as role models. It is the drug dealers who are able to provide for their families, drive nice cars and wear nice clothes. They are seen by many as a symbol of success.

The users, or customers, in this drug trade may be lured by what seems to be a carefree lifestyle or, perhaps, in drugs they see a temporary escape from their grim surroundings. It can be a devastating cycle in which crime, violence and deception play a large part. Many of these people eventually find themselves in trouble with the law.

Others might begin using drugs or alcohol recreationally. It is virtually considered a right of passage for teenagers and college students to experiment with alcohol for social reasons. They might begin to drink or even do drugs for weekend fun, but many move toward dependency. They might imbibe in celebration but also drown their sorrows. Eventually, they might use drugs or alcohol just to get through the day. It is the abuse of alcohol or drugs that can lead to dependency and, as many inmates contend, it is dependency that can turn you into someone else. Logic, concern and consequences, inmates have said, matter little when your every action revolves around drugs or alcohol.

It is unfortunate to think that for some people prison offers refuge from this kind of life. It is at the same time encouraging to know that where such programs exist, people will benefit. Only the most fortunate of the inmates whom I met through the Gateway program moved on to penitentiaries where they were able to continue their work in a drug program.

It has been said by many that embracing God is most frequently the only cure for the most severe addicts. Indeed, the founders of Alcoholics Anonymous, with their Christian-based approach to healing, carry the same belief. In releasing their problem to a "higher power," addicts may in fact be replacing the pleasure of drugs and alcohol with the more fulfilling pleasure of experiencing God.

Eddie is one inmate who I believe epitomizes the change one can make when you discover the perfect blend of taking and receiving — taking personal responsibility for yourself and receiving the love of God. Perhaps he is also a tragic case study for the leaders of Alcoholics Anonymous.

Upon entering the [Cook] County jail I was in a very desperate condition. With a sober mind, the horrible realization of what I did and my whole past was staring me in the face. Drugs and alcohol weren't available for me to escape reality. All my thoughts were consumed with what I did. I wanted to die but was too afraid to kill myself. For the first time in my life I feared that if I did kill myself, after the crime I committed, I would surely go to hell. I had never felt so bad in my life. I was stuck in the middle of being too afraid to live and too afraid to die by my own hand. I had reached my ultimate bottom.

For the first couple weeks I was kept on suicide watch because of the state of mind I was in. Out of pure desperation I got on my knees and cried my heart out to God for forgiveness. . . . If anything, I was begging God to take my life. Knowing that I had committed the worst crime imaginable, I couldn't stand living in my own skin. I can't say that after crying out to God that I felt any comfort or spiritual reassurance. Somehow, though, out of all the confusion and depression, I knew that I had better just keep crying out . . . I guess I thought that if I stopped reaching out to God I would undoubtedly go crazy or kill myself.

As I began coming to my senses, I was taken off the suicide watch and taken to one of the buildings in the jail to await trial. It was then that I started attending worship services and reading the Bible and any other spiritual literature that I could get my hands on. At one of these services I met and got acquainted with Sister Josephine. While Sister Josephine ran the Christian service, I listened intently as she talked about the love and forgiveness of Jesus. I broke down crying just about every time. It wasn't anything that I hadn't heard though. My mother was telling me about Jesus' love and forgiveness since I got arrested.

I felt very comfortable with Sister Josephine. I told her about my crime and how sorry I was. In no time I was sharing my whole life with her. Sister then gave me some advice that I never forgot. She told me to seek out and participate in all the positive things that I can.

Eddie applied for and was accepted into a drug program located in the dorm in which he was being housed. This program was much smaller than the Gateway program of Division #8. Perhaps that was the place for Eddie to start, for this was the first small but important step in what continues to be a long way back from Eddie's horrible beginnings.

Eddie says his father was an alcoholic who abused his mother for many years. "I have painful memories of my mother crying from all the pains of our lives," he wrote. "I swore I would never become a drunk like my father. . . . I would tell my ma that I was going to buy her a nice house when I got older."

His story is not unlike many others I have heard about those who grow up under the same roof with an alcoholic. Eddie did follow in the ways of his father. At an early age he began drinking alcohol and smoking marijuana. He soon became lost in his own world. When his parents were divorced, he said it was like a "license to run wild."

The party life continued, but rather than feeling confident and alive, drugs and alcohol began to tear him down. He dropped out of high school his sophomore year. One night, after getting drunk and high, he and a girlfriend decided to jump off of a building. Eddie said they had hoped to go to heaven together. He broke a few bones but his girlfriend died.

> Just as soon as I came out of intensive care I resumed getting high right in the hospital bed. I didn't discuss my feelings about my dead girlfriend with anyone, telling my friends never to bring up her name. My way of dealing with things was not to deal with them at all. In my family feelings weren't discussed. All I knew was to hold them in.

Eddie's life continued to spiral downward. He soon fathered a child with a new girlfriend, but only saw his son a few times before the boy was taken away from the mother by the Department of Children and Family Services (DCFS). "I made no attempt at all to take care of that child," he said. "Sure it bothered me, but I just drank and drugged my conscience away. . . ."

A few years later he became a father again. He was excited and saw this as a second chance.

I loved my girlfriend and wanted a baby by her. I thought for sure that by becoming a father I would automatically become responsible and that my life would finally straighten out.

Besides the doctor, I was the first one to see God's miracle, my son, enter this world. I was sober and filled with so much emotion that I was almost trembling. When the doctor lifted him up his eyes were wide open and he seemed to be smiling at me. I smiled back, with tears of overwhelming love pouring down my face. I was awestruck. He was just like a miniature version of me.

Immediately after leaving the birthing room I ran to the visitors room where some of my family was. Still flooded with emotions I let my family know that my son was born. . . . It was at this time, while experiencing all these emotions, that I got the most overwhelming obsession for alcohol that I can remember. This desire to drink was so uncomfortable because I felt good feeling what I was feeling. Then I started feeling guilty because I wanted a drink so bad that it was driving me crazy . . .

In the past I always felt like a bad person when I desired a drink at inappropriate times. When my son was born, I felt bad that me wanting a drink had something to do with my love or lack of love for him . . .

I thought that I would change for him. But, I didn't know at the time that the obsession to drink and drug had a mental control over me. I still believed that I was the one that controlled when I wanted to use and how much.

Eddie wasn't getting better. He began to steal from the hardware store where he worked. For extra money he would take scrap metal and aluminum cans to the junk yard. Then he began breaking into apartment buildings to steal the brass plumbing fixtures and cast iron radiators. He said he purposely didn't marry his girlfriend so she could collect food stamps and government aid. "At one point," he said, "I drained my mother of everything she had. I convinced her I needed the money for my son."

When he was fired from his job, Eddie checked into a 21-day drug rehabilitation clinic but later relapsed with alcohol and cocaine. His girlfriend told him she had had enough, she was taking their baby and leaving. At 25 years old he was once again living with his mother.

Eventually, Eddie latched on to another girlfriend and moved into her apartment with her 2-year-old boy. She held a full-time job and Eddie thought of her as responsible.

Outwardly, things seemed to be going pretty smooth . . . I was working a respectable amount of hours as a laborer. Quite often when I got home from work my girlfriend would be going to work. Because I cared for her child very much, the baby attached himself to me right from the beginning. She trusted me to baby-sit while she worked. . . . I really drew close to her baby because he was only a few months younger than my son. My son's mother would sometimes drop my son off to visit where I was staying . . .

I continued to baby-sit . . . while I was drinking and drugging. I started feeling trapped. Here I was baby-sitting someone else's child and I couldn't even take care of my own child. I hated myself. Every time my son would leave from a visit, I would break down when nobody was around. I was drinking and getting high as much as I could in an attempt to suppress my feelings. But the drugs and alcohol didn't work anymore. All they did was contribute to my breaking point.

I went from loving and caring for [my girlfriend's child] to being mean and abusive to him. . . . For one and a half weeks the abuse continued and progressed until the night when he fell unconscious and died because of my abuse. What happened was I put a stuffed animal over his face in an attempt to stop his crying after causing him to cry by yelling and hitting him.

The very moment the child fell unconscious I snapped out of the abusive state and tried to revive him through CPR. I tried again while on the phone with 911 emergency. It was too late. He never woke up.

Even at the height of the abuse, it was never my intention to kill him. It never, not even for a moment, crossed my mind. The life of a perfectly innocent child was gone. And I was charged with first degree murder.

There is nothing easy about forgiveness. When the life of another is so senselessly taken, we must as a society take action to protect ourselves from further danger. We must enforce consequences for such behavior, but we must not return torture with torture, trade one death for another.

No matter what strides Eddie makes in overcoming his illness, he will never truly recover from the devastating and permanent results of his actions — this is part of his punishment. But his punishment is also a challenge. He must live with what he has done, but live he must. And forgive, we must. As he is challenged to find meaning in his life, we are challenged to find forgiveness in our hearts. If we are to honor our pact with God, we are bound as well to find meaning in Eddie's life. As I asserted earlier, this may be our ultimate test.

In choosing to live with purpose, Eddie has chosen to accept responsibility. He has also chosen to accept his punishment rather than to wallow in it or be destroyed by it. As a society, we are encouraged to learn from Eddie and he from us.

Jumping both feet into recovery, I followed Sister Josephine's advice, getting involved in everything I could to better myself and my situation. I sought out and received individual therapy from one of the counselors. It was in this private therapy that I got in touch and had a chance to release feelings that were eating away at my guts. I learned what it meant to trust a person completely. I shared all my deep secrets, letting all the skeletons out of the closet. . . . As embarrassing as it was, I discussed all my sex issues and hang-ups. I talked about my relationships with my girl-friends, family, other friends and people in general. We talked in-depth about my crime, my son and the son I never took care of. I did a lot of crying in these sessions. I also did some laughing. My life wasn't all sadness and misery.

Most of all though, I left those therapy sessions feeling giant burdens were lifted. I prayed to God before and after each session, thanking Him for the courage to keep me pushing forward.

. . . Unlike the time in the rehab-hospital on the streets, this time I was willing to accept and acknowledge that I was powerless over alcohol and drugs. . . . I listened intently to the crazy things [the group leaders and other participants] spoke about doing in their past while under the influence and how they turned their lives around by working the pro-gram and believing in a Higher Power.

It was there, at these meetings, that my Higher Power started coming alive and having meaning to me. . . . I choose to believe that my Higher Power is Jesus Christ.

. . . Prayer started becoming a regular part of my life. The more I prayed the more I began asking God to help me trust Him with my life. As I listened to others share their stories it dawned on me that God was working through their honesty to help me make sense out of my past. As some of my fears slowly drifted away I realized that God could restore me to a healthy state of mind and body. I knew then that recovery for me meant doing everything in my power to help myself and trusting that God will bless my efforts.

Eddie's recovery program was eventually integrated into the much larger Gateway program, which puts more focus on behav-ior modification. For the first time he was looking at himself and his addiction from a new perspective. In my continued meetings with him during this time, I noticed a dramatic change in his demeanor. He was much more upbeat, confident and even looked much healthier. The enthusiasm with which he approached each aspect of his recovery was quite remarkable.

> . . . I learned alot about how I relate to others. I learned alot about my strange habits and mannerisms. I also learned so much about how I could be of help to others and society instead of a menace. I liked this [Gateway] program so much because we had more meetings with more outside volunteers each week. Being that I was in this program so long while awaiting trial, I held just about every job function there was, some of them twice.
>
> For a long time it was my job to chair the meetings. I prayed for and God gave me the courage to speak in front of a group that was almost 100 people sometimes.
>
> Again, following Sister's advice, I sought out and received one year of intense therapy from the intern pathologist. Together we explored my childhood, my choices as a child, the abuse, etc. Mainly what I learned there was how I carried most of my childhood thinking into my adult life. Understanding is the key to knowledge, so this therapy helped me quite a bit.
>
> . . . I started writing a journal. Each night I'd briefly write my thoughts, feelings and events of the day. This helped put the day's happenings in perspective. It also helped keep me aware of my progression or back-sliding. At the end of each section of the journal I would write a prayer to God. I poured my heart out in quite a few of those prayers, crying out for help and thanking Him for what He has already done.
>
> . . . Reading also became a major tool for my mind. I knew how to read from learning in grade school. But only until I entered jail did I read my first book cover to cover. At the time it was the greatest accomplishment ever. It was a Christian recovery book about a family that overcame the power that alcoholism had over them. From there I read every spiritual and/or recovery book that I could get my

hands on. My whole life my mother had been telling me how important books are. Well, now I know.

Eddie also became involved in a pen-pal program between other AA members — both in prison and out. He says that along with his mother, who has always stood by him, these pen-pals gave him people to love and care for and also served to remind him that he was loved and cared for.

As Eddie continued to show signs of progress, his case was still being dragged out in court. Being charged with first degree murder meant the state set out to prove Eddie's crime was intentional and pre-meditated. Fearful that if convicted in the first degree Eddie would receive a natural life sentence or the death penalty, his lawyer settled the case. Eddie was sentenced to 50 years. With good behavior, Eddie will conceivably have to serve 25 years.

After getting my time I went back to the drug unit to say good-bye to my friends. I spoke at one of my last meetings, letting everybody know that with God's help I have accepted my time, and that I'm trusting God to take care and protect me in the penitentiary.

Down I went to the penitentiary with a bag full of spiritual tools that I had acquired from the drug program and all the therapy. I knew that I had to trust in God or I would be quickly consumed and overwhelmed with fear and all other sorts of negative thoughts. I also knew that the second I got off the bus I had to jump right into what ever worship services, therapy groups, and other positive activities were available. And so I did.

I met and got acquainted with the chaplain as soon as I got there. I put in request slips to him for one-on-one spiritual counseling. I let him know my love for God's will instead of my own. We quickly became friends. I also attended and participated in two worship services.

Another request slip went to the psychologist. I got involved in one-on-one with him and also group therapy for substance abusers. Speaking openly and honestly, I fit right in. . . . Recovery continued as I reached out to meet new people and make new friends. While using alcohol and drugs I used to feel that I was so different from everybody else. But after being involved in so many recovery groups I found out that most of us users and abusers are basically the same. We all have basically the same problems and have done most of the same insane things while using, in varying degrees.

Wasting no time at all I jumped into school. Both in and out of class I studied day and night for my GED. The hard work paid off as it usually does. I received my GED certificate within the first few months of incarceration. It was only through constant prayer and God's help that I was able to concentrate and study for that test like I did. I had so many doubts and fears while studying for and taking the test. But I kept praying and God helped me to stay focused in spite of my doubts and fears. After completing my GED I managed to finish and get credited for one college class before all colleges were taken out of maximum security institutions.

Feeling disappointed that I couldn't continue with college, I used to painfully fantasize about how long it would take to make it to medium security where I could continue college. I found out that one of the GED teachers had just started a typing class, and so I joined. After a few months and countless hours of practice, I learned to type sufficiently without looking at the keys. Because I had very low self-esteem, learning to type was something that I never thought in a million years I would be able to accomplish. It's now a reality.

A new law was just recently passed where inmates with 20 years or less, with a good record, could get in to medium security. It just so happened that this law came into effect exactly at the same time that I got under 20 years. I have never received a ticket and my record is spotless. So I was one of the very first people to get taken out of max-security.

Now it is also possible for me to continue in college. I'm already signed up . . .

While Eddie has many years left to serve, he looks forward only to the day ahead of him. In all the years of my ministry, I have encountered no other inmate with such unflinching dedication to his spiritual and emotional awakening. He often seems immune to the natural highs and lows experienced by those incarcerated for any significant length of time. Perhaps this is due in part to his inclination to reach out to others.

I regularly receive letters from inmates — who had met Eddie at Cook County jail — asking me to send him their regards and to let him know how helpful he has been to them. Some who have wound up at the same penitentiary with Eddie tell me how much of an inspiration he continues to be. One man wrote, "Sister, I am continually amazed by Eddie's enduring spirit." Some men who have been released from prison continue to write to Eddie in search of advice or just to keep their friendship alive.

Acting as a supportive friend to others and sharing the word of God, Eddie says, is part of his recovery and part of his duty. In prison, of all places, Eddie seems to have discovered a new way to live, and a new person to love.

. . . The only way I'm able to do this amount of time and keep my sanity is by trusting that if I keep doing the right things for the right reasons God will open doors and a bright future will unfold. I live one day at a time doing what needs to be done to improve my relationship with God, with myself and the people around me. I get great pleasure out of helping people instead of hurting them. Whenever I do something to improve or better my life I grow as a person. . . .

God has brought me so far from the person I used to be. I quit smoking over four and a half years ago, and haven't had a drink or drug for over five years. That's a miracle! My suggestion to anyone who wants to turn their life around is the same suggestion that Sister Josephine gave me over five years ago in the County jail. Seek out and get involved in anything and everything that's positive while at the same time trusting that God will for sure bless your efforts.

I have witnessed Eddie's transformation and am grateful to have been of help to him. Of course, his recovery is a daily process and he has a long road ahead. He may find his greatest challenge down that long road, on the day of his eventual release. He now lives in preparation for that day, when he can freely apply his newfound love of self, others and God in the world outside his prison cell.

Perhaps Eddie's story and that of inmates like him offers support to new ideas of how we punish and attempt to rehabilitate those who have sinned against society. With thoughts of a more therapeutic approach to incarceration, I am reminded of an experience Charles "Chuck" Colson shared at a conference I was fortunate enough to attend.

Chuck Colson served as Special Counsel to President Richard Nixon's administration before pleading guilty and serving jail time for his actions in the Watergate scandal. Upon his release, Colson declared himself a Born-Again Christian and, much to the surprise of his critics, has served as an activist for the rights of prisoners and prison reform ever since.

Colson said his time in jail opened his eyes to the plight of prisoners everywhere, that he was struck by the human degradation and the fact that most inmates had "nothing to live for and no place to go and nothing to care about." The only sign of hope he saw in prison was the fellowship of those who shared their faith in Christ. In looking for some way to help inmates, Colson founded his Prison Fellowship. In fact, he was awarded the coveted Templeton Award in 1993 for his work. The award is given once a year to honor progress in religion and includes a $1 million donation to the winner's cause.

When I learned Colson would receive this award in Chicago at the Conference of World Religions, I was determined to be there. I was moved by his eloquent speech and its revolutionary vision of prison reform. The concept he spoke of teaches that freedom is found in submission to a moral law. It says that duty is our sharpest weapon against fear and tyranny. This revolution, Colson said, raises an unchanging and eternal moral standard, and offers hope to everyone who fails to reach it. It sets the content of justice, and transforms the will to achieve it. It builds communities of character and of compassion.

Colson also recounted an experience that was quite inspiring. "On occasion," he said, "God provides glimpses of His glory. I witnessed one in an unlikely place, a prison in Brazil, like none that I've ever seen." He went on to say:

> *As one who has served time in prison, and has since spent most of my life working in them, I'll never forget the most unusual prison I've ever visited.*
>
> *Called Humaita Prison, it is in São José dos Campos in Brazil. Formerly a government prison, it is now operated by Prison Fellowship Brazil as an alternative prison, without armed guards or high-tech security. Instead, it is run on the Christian principles of love of God and respect for men.*
>
> *Humaita has only two full-time staff; the rest of the work is done by 730 inmates serving time for everything from murder and assault to robbery and drug-related crimes. Every man is assigned another inmate to whom he is accountable. In addition, each prisoner is assigned a volunteer mentor from the outside who works with him during his term and after his release. Prisoners take classes on character development and are encouraged to participate in educational and religious programs.*
>
> *When I visited this prison, I found the inmates smiling — particularly the murderer who held the keys, opened the gates and let me in. Wherever I walked I saw men at peace. I saw clean living areas. I saw people working industriously. The walls were decorated with motivational sayings and Scripture.*
>
> *Humaita has an astonishing record. Its recidivism rate is 4 percent, compared to 75 percent in the rest of Brazil. How is that possible?*

I saw the answer when my inmate guide escorted me to the notorious cell once used for solitary punishment. Today, he told me, it always houses the same inmate. As we reached the end of the long, concrete corridor and he put the key into the lock, he paused and asked, "Are you sure you want to go in?"

"Of course," I replied. "I've been in isolation cells all over the world." Slowly he swung open the massive door, and I saw the prisoner in that cell: a crucifix, beautifully carved — Jesus, hanging on the cross.

"He's doing time for the rest of us," my guide said softly.

With this philosophy in mind, Colson has built an organization that, much like the programs based on Alcoholics Anonymous, works in prisons across the country. A staff of nearly 100 work at the organization's headquarters near Washington, D.C. Their primary job is to assist the more than 12,000 volunteers who carry out the ministry. These volunteers represent all denominations and walks of life. They include Catholic nuns, Baptist pastors, doctors, truck drivers, police officers and even one 97-year-old widow. They evangelize in the prisons, write letters to prison pen pals, lead Bible studies, help newly released prisoners find jobs and homes, provide help for prisoner's family or simply offer prayer for the inmates.

A headline in the January 16, 1998 issue of the Chicago Tribune *read: "Texas inmates, jailers sing praises of Christian-based program." The article went on to describe how Colson's organization took over and now runs the entire wing of the facility in a church-state cooperation, which was the first time that the system has allowed a private, Christian organization to do so. The ministry accepted inmates with the last 18 months before their release dates — with no extra cost to the state beyond the housing, food, and guards it already provides. Texas Governor George W. Bush, who strongly supports this idea, visited the wing with Colson and even joined the inmate choir in singing "Amazing Grace."*

The article said it will be at least three years before officials know whether the program is working to reduce the system's prison recidivism rate, which now runs at about 48 percent. But, according to the article, inmates, top prison officials and church volunteers say they already believe it is changing minds. It quoted one inmate as saying, "Most of us here sincerely want to change, I know I do." A prison guard added, "I've already seen changes in [the inmates'] habits and attitude. . . . When you get a group of inmates of different cultures and backgrounds to study together and to read the Bible together, it's going to make a difference."

Many of the inmates I met at Cook County were fortunate to encounter the work of Colson's ministry in other prisons. One wrote to me to describe the experience.

I am just bursting with joy in the Lord, after a weekend, three-day Christian seminar [here]. Our theme was, "loving others." The small group in which I was blessed included a facilitator who's love of Jesus and knowledge of the Holy Sprit just leaped in to me. She has several years in prison ministry and has opened herself to God to be used in whatever way needed. The theme was and is so beautiful and needed.

[Their] worship and singing were on target. The program was sponsored by Chuck Colson's Christian prison ministry. We have 20 volunteers, each working with 30 men. There are 400 men here, but 30 men willing to admit and share Christ in open worship is great. Please include the volunteers in this ministry in your prayers and include our inmates and me too.

Chuck Colson is a splendid example of what can happen once you turn your life over to God. Rather than being quieted by those who doubted his transformation, Colson has let his actions stand as testimony to his commitment.

10

A Blessed Ministry

Sister Josephine stands at the podium, her head bowed in prayer. The men also bow their heads, some covering their faces with their palms and others folding their hands in their laps. Sister recites a special prayer and once again reiterates God's love for them all. "In Him," she concludes, "you will find your greatest strength. Now go in peace."

The men stand and, although a few file out of the recreation room, the others begin forming a line around Sister's display table. They pick up religious booklets, rosaries and candy and await a private moment with Sister. One by one she offers them a few words and a warm hug.

The room empties and Sister Josephine begins packing up the materials that remain. It's close to 3 p.m. and her day here is done.

When I reflect on the many years of my prison ministry, I look back in thanks and praise to two people in particular: my own mother and St. Frances Xavier Cabrini.

My mother, Theresa, was a hard working person who sacrificed herself for her family and her neighbors. She reared ten children while helping my father in a meat market in New Jersey.

When I was a few months old, my family went to Italy. My uncle needed my father's help for a time, but soon tried to persuade him to remain in Italy for good. "My children are American, and that is where we shall return," my mother exclaimed. And we did.

My father returned home to prepare a house for us, leaving my mother and seven children at the time to return by boat. It took us 20 days to travel from Italy to New York City. When the customs officer saw all us children and our trunks, he was overwhelmed and told us to "just pass through."

My love for the water was born on that ship, although I was punished for going out on deck amid a great storm. Of course, I was soaked by a terrific wave.

When I was eight years old my mother became deathly ill and was not expected to live. Without any prompting I prayed silently before a large picture of St. Therese, the Little Flower. "Please," I prayed, "don't let my mother die. If she lives I will become a sister." At the time I hadn't the faintest idea what that entailed, and my mother recovered.

My mother received little education but had a keen intuition. She always knew when something was awry, always knew when she was needed. She served as an interpreter for some of the neighbors who couldn't speak English. My mother was caring and hospitable to all types and ages of people, but she also knew how to practice "tough love." She gave and gave without counting the cost.

I shall never forget my trip to the Novitiate for the first time. As I sat next to my mother in the car, she took my cold hand and placed it next to her heart. I did not realize I was not only receiving the warmth of her touch, but her silent love as we rode along. My mother influenced my life so much that I considered my prison ministry a privilege, not a chore. I feel her presence always.

I was 16 when I graduated high school and, like my sister, Sr. Innocent, my great desire was to enter the convent. My sister and I learned about Mother Cabrini through a priest and at age 22 my sister entered the Missionary Sisters of the Sacred Heart, founded by Mother Cabrini. To my great relief, I was able to enter the following year.

It was the knowledge of Mother Cabrini's work that spurred me to join this order so many years ago, and to do my best to help continue the work she began.

In the early part of this century Mother Cabrini not only worked in poor neighborhoods of Chicago, but she used her influence and leadership to reach out to prisoners across the country. She appointed several sisters to the special work of visiting inmates two or three times a week.

In Chicago, the sisters held a weekly catechism class where abject prisoners were able to learn about the teachings of God and were helped in seeing how those teachings can apply to their own lives. In Denver, where the sisters walked great miles through the snow to reach a prison, the inmates, staff and officials gave the sisters a gift of a horse and carriage to help ease their travel.

As an Italian, one of Mother Cabrini's great concerns was the lack of an Italian-speaking Catholic chaplain for the prisoners in Sing Sing, a penitentiary in upstate New York. With her characteristic determination she saw that they got one, instructing her sisters in Manhattan to send their own chaplain to minister to the men.

A beautiful relationship developed between Mother Cabrini and the Sing Sing prisoners. A representative of the Italian inmates wrote to welcome her back in 1902 after her sojourn to Italy. She responded with a warm and loving letter, which was published in its entirety in the Sing Sing bi-weekly newspaper. Mother Cabrini addressed the inmates as "miei buoni amici," (my dear friends). She singled out their simple letter of welcome to her and complimented the men for their fine, Italian composition, their gentle sentiments and the goodness of their hearts. Mother Cabrini believed that she was not speaking to hardened criminals, but to her brothers. She told them that even when she was far away, her prayers were with them, and that she was always interested to receive news of their good conduct.

What pleasure these dejected prisoners must have felt when Mother Cabrini wrote, "I would very much like to visit you, to thank you personally for all that you have done for me." And she did.

In gratitude, the inmates of Sing Sing responded in kind for all the sisters had done for them. On the occasion of the Silver Jubilee of our Institute, the Missionary Sisters of the Sacred Heart, they produced a laudatory testimonial that included a detailed account of all that had been done for them. All the prisoners signed their names and it was sent to Mother Cabrini.

In one of these letters there is an account of an Italian man condemned to die. Barely 29 years of age, the man insisted he was not guilty, and the sisters tried to help him. They presented a plea to the governor of New York and were able to obtain a stay for one month. The sisters also made it possible for the inmate's son, who was being raised in an orphanage run by the sisters, to visit his father in his cell. It seemed that because of newly admitted evidence in his favor, the young prisoner had real hope of being freed.

He was later informed that his sentence was fixed, and his execution would be carried out. The man planned to commit suicide, but the sisters continued to support him and prepare him for what was to come. On the day of his death he was resigned to his fate.

God did nothing evil, so why was He sentenced to life on the cross? Good people remained silent in the face of injustice and ingratitude. They lacked the courage to speak out, to rock the boat like Mother Cabrini and her sisters did. We must not continue condemning Christ anew in the persons of the poor, the youth or prisoners by doing nothing while the enemies of Christ keep crucifying Him. An inmate has written:

> I remember you saying it's not easy to have strong faith. And I know doubts and questions seep into my faith. I keep telling myself if it weren't for God, I would most likely be dead right now.

You and I may not have much to give, but we can share a smile, or a listening ear, or a kind word, or a visit to someone who is ill. We can write a letter or make a phone call and pray for those in difficulty. We can also reach out to inmates.

Prisoners welcome three forms of help. First, write them letters. Volunteers don't even need to leave home to bring some sense of the Gospel to inmates. Volunteers who know no one in prison can contact a prison service organization or a prison chaplain in order to be matched up with an inmate.

Second, if your letter writing results in a safe, comfortable and appropriate relationship, consider talking with inmates by phone. Recent court orders have offered telephone usage to almost all prisoners. Volunteers can talk to an inmate on the phone if they are willing to accept the charges. Many prisoners have no one besides a volunteer to call.

Third, as a comfortable relationship progresses, consider making a visit to a prisoner. Again, consult with a prison service organization or prison chaplain to learn more about the procedures of visitation. If you want to take it further, you might decide to conduct prayer groups or tutor the illiterate. Listen to them, pray with them and become family to them.

We punish them when they violate a trust, but we must also continue to see them and love them as God does. An inmate has written:

> Before you came into my life, I didn't believe anyone had faith in me or loved me. Many people have given up on me because I could no longer fulfill their selfish needs. Moreover, love and friendship have usually been conditional. You, on the other hand, have shown me what God's love really looks like and feels like. . . . I think the Lord planned that our paths must cross, and I pray for a lasting friendship.

Contained in the life stories of many of the inmates in my care are incidents of abuse — physical, moral and sexual — by parents or by members of their family or friends. The abuse and punishment of their childhood carries over into their adult behavior and leaves them with little self-esteem. If you are to serve as a volunteer in this capacity, don't fortify their negativity. Separate those determined to improve themselves from those not desiring of making the necessary changes in their conduct and thinking. Mixing the two groups exposes the potentially good to the negative influence of the obstinate ones.

Ministry opportunities don't end at the jail. Many prisoners have left family members behind in wait. These family members also face a need for love and concern at a critical time as they too feel the emotional strain that comes with an arrest, a trial, and incarceration. Many relatives, in a sense, feel imprisoned with their loved ones. Marriages come under a terrible strain. The survival of a marriage could depend on the kind of support a volunteer can lend.

Almost every city or large political subdivision has a local jail that may lack a significant prison outreach. Such jails are temporary holding facilities used to detain men and women awaiting trials or hearings. Many of the jails are old, overcrowded and dirty. The first-time arrest or incarceration will occasionally jolt a new offender into a new reevaluation of life. This is an excellent time for a Christian visitor to have a major influence.

Clare Booth Luce defines a Christian as someone who embodies the spirit of Jesus. When a stranger comes up to a Christian on the street merely to ask the time of day, that stranger can tell from your voice, from the smile on your lips and from the gleam in your eye that the Lord lives within you. This is the good news, and this is why Christ founded the church. We help with our words, but at the deepest level, we help with who we are.

Prison ministry is an answer to the urgent call from Jesus to see and meet Him in others, in whom it is sometimes difficult to see the hand of God at work. To make the Gospel alive, we must look at the presence of Jesus, as He portrays Himself in the smallest and meekest among us.

In the 25th chapter of St. Matthew's Gospel, Jesus said, "Come ye, blessed of my Father, possess the kingdom prepared for you from the foundation of the world. Because I was hungry and you gave me to eat, I was thirsty and you gave me to drink, I was sick and imprisoned and you visited me, I was naked and you clothed me, I was a stranger and you took me in, then will come the greatest revelation. What you did to those around me, you did it to me."

Broken hearts are strewn all around us, and they can be healed only by love, by the kindness that you and I can give, we who say we believe. Believe me, I learned more from the inmates than I could ever give, you too will receive great recompense here and in the hereafter from inmates and then from God himself. An inmate has written:

> I would like to take this time to say I appreciate all the understanding, love and special help you have given me over the years. Without you there to give me moral and spiritual support, I would have lost my mind and suffered a great deal more. . . . Your words have helped me in many ways and have showed me that God is kind and loving toward me. I know I could have been judged much harsher by man, but through Christ I was saved because only He knows my heart and soul.

It is true that ministering to the incarcerated can be quite demanding and presents many surprises — not all of them welcome. However, any lay person can work through their faith communities and governmental avenues to help make our society more like the Kingdom of God, a kingdom which acknowledges the need for justice but which is founded upon the mercy and salvation of Jesus Christ — Himself once a convicted felon.

We should ponder often, why did God make me? To know Him, to love Him and to serve Him in this world, and to be happy with Him in this world, and certainly in the next.

If our minds are so unloving, so ignoble, so unlike the mind of Christ, then we cannot be taken into heaven, because in heaven there is nothing but love. I pray that many of you who read this book will be inspired to dedicate some time to this ministry. However, I realize not everyone has the qualifications, time or disposition for an effective prison ministry. All of us, however, can make a difference in the world simply by practicing and demonstrating our faith.

Society is marked by broken families, the unjust distribution of wealth and a frightening disregard for the value of human life. Every family, every individual is called to follow Jesus and to trust in Him. Do we believe that when we trust in Him, He can accomplish the impossible? He can use us to change the entire world. If we spend time with Him in prayer He will press His word upon our hearts and fill us with a desire to share His word with everyone. God wants all of His children to be prophets in their own lives, bold yet humble proclaimers of His word.

Parents, for example, are called to be prophetic voices to their children, and husbands and wives should always be willing to give and receive God's word to each other. Teachers, workers, citizens and neighbors are all called to speak God's life-giving word. Let His spirit speak to you. He will give you the love and wisdom to say those things He wants to have said in a way that will bear fruit. Don't let fear hold you back.

Many inmates are now in jail and prison in part because they lacked humble yet Christian role models. Become positive role models by keeping away from drugs, alcohol, violence and gangs. Vote intelligently on issues such as drug and gun control. Adopt a family member, a neighbor, a young person in need and offer your help. Pray for the individual, befriend him, take him out occasionally. Help a young person with homework and do what your loving heart inspires you to do.

For those who are ministers to inmates already, you have undoubtedly experienced the concerns, frustrations, difficulties and perhaps even fears or doubts that are part of the journey. But you also know the joy, satisfaction and inner peace of witnessing the Lord's return for lost sheep, His reunion with His prodigal sons and daughters, and the healing of lives which much of society often leaves for dead. It is the promise of these resurrections that must inspire us to avoid losing God's connection in the taxing aspects of this work.

On top of that, as strange as it may seem to some, those who minister to inmates are not above suspicion. There are countless eyes and ears focused in our direction by both correctional staff and inmates. In this atmosphere it is essential that we conduct ourselves in a manner above reproach and in accordance with Christ at all times. We must always let the Holy Spirit be our guide. We are role models and ambassadors to Christ but our commitment and trustworthiness will continually be tested. The Gospel will be tested as well, by those yearning to discover whether the Lord possesses the power of transformation and salvation. An inmate has written:

> There is one thing I have learned from this ordeal. And that is there is truly an Almighty God, up or down there, that really cares about human beings who are afflicted. . . . As I trust in God, my faith is strengthened.

What better testing ground is there than jail or prison? Our loving and all-powerful God is up to the challenge. We simply need to be humble, responsible, obedient and merciful servants for Him and to Him. Seeing the water in our midst turn to wine (John 2:1–11) is one of the many blessings God imparts to us in jail and prison. It is a blessing which we are constantly challenged and inspired to assist and witness.

Few people have assisted and witnessed more in prison than the members of Kolbe House, a Chicago-based Christian organization dedicated to affecting prison policy and aiding those incarcerated and released from prison. It is the Kolbe House that helps ministers like me gain access to correctional centers like Cook County. The organization works closely with inmates of Cook County jail and the Audy Home, a correctional institute for juvenile offenders, as well as other Illinois prisons.

Relying on its Christian principles and its personal relationships with inmates, Kolbe House develops recommendations that it hopes will improve the prison system for both inmates and authorities. Its influence with the state has already proven effective in keeping alive the concept of rehabilitation in a climate that often seems determined to concentrate solely on punishment.

Just last year, Kolbe House was instrumental in the optimistic provisions contained in a report released by the Illinois Department of Corrections Performance Review Panel, which is made up of prison administrators. Among other positive recommendations, the panel suggested that the Department of Corrections pilot a gang-free prison for medium-security inmates to curb the rise in prison gang activity. It also set forth a strategy to reduce the waiting list for and include more inmates in its educational programs, to expand the prison system's Life Skills Curriculum — which would include components such as violence reduction and domestic violence reduction, moral reasoning skills and victim awareness — and reevaluate its vocational training so that it would be relevant to today's working world. The panel also suggested expanding the substance abuse programs and establishing a network of community-based drug reintegration programs.

The invaluable services performed by Kolbe House includes serving as a constant reminder that we as a society should never be satisfied with a prison population that continues to rise. Now, with more than 41,000 people imprisoned in Illinois — compared with just over 20,000 in 1988 — Kolbe House preaches that prison reform must always be a top priority. It continually stresses the fact that the majority of the incarcerated will someday be released; that all inmates are not the same (despite the focus of the media, a substantial percentage of prisoners are convicted of nonviolent crimes); and that the many illiterate inmates who enter the system are also illiterate when they are released to society. The organization's pro-active approach works toward one primary goal, which was eloquently stated by George W. Brooks in a recent issue of the Kolbe House newsletter: "We urge the human treatment of inmates combined with reasonable efforts for rehabilitation, education and job training. Billions of dollars are spent on building and maintaining prisons. It is beyond dispute that it is more cost-efficient to educate and rehabilitate than it is to incarcerate. Punitive treatment is not a deterrent . . . Our communities will be safer when inmates are released with a change of attitude and the skills and ability to obtain jobs that offer a living wage.

Judges, legislators and prison officials would be smart to consider more seriously the recommendations made by Christian organizations like Kolbe House, spiritual directors like Sister Helen Prejean and nationally respected activists like Chuck Colson.

For those of you who are ministers or would like to learn more about ministering to inmates, the Kolbe House is an organization that would like to be introduced to you.

For those men and women who are currently in jail or prison, at this very moment begin to seek God and follow Jesus. As difficult as your surroundings and circumstances may seem or actually be, open yourself up to the changing power of the Holy Spirit and use whatever length of time you must serve as a spiritual retreat.

Seek out any positive activities that are available to you. Attend worship services regularly and start or renew a daily prayer life. Take this time to study Sacred Scripture and inspirational writings and consider how these writings apply to you and your life. Familiarize yourself with the lives of the saints who have come before you, keeping in mind that many men and women have been imprisoned for a variety of reasons since the beginning of this world. God was willing and able to heal, guide and use all of them. You are no exception to God's desire or ability.

Further, use this time to avail yourself to any programs which will help prepare you for your future — even if you may never leave prison in this life. Participate in alcohol and drug abuse sessions, marriage and family workshops, adult basic education classes, high school equivalency programs, vocational training courses, college courses and anything else which will help you, your family and society. Governments do not rehabilitate inmates, but God can . . . with your help, hard work and dedication. An inmate has written:

If we just hear His words and don't do anything with them, we deceive ourselves. We forget what manner of man we are. We forget who we are in Christ and the power of His word. We will deceive ourselves by trying to reason things out contrary to the word. But when we look into the perfect law of liberty (The Word) and continue therein being a doer, we shall be blessed in all our deeds.

This is your time to read, to listen, to pray, to learn, and to be remade into the type of person Our Lord calls all of us to be. The time will come for you to preach, to teach, and to testify but, for now, let your actions be all of those things. Let your actions and your example be the revelation of the true power of the Gospel, as Jesus showed all of us by His example. Let your good works and behavior give glory to God so that all may see Christ's light (Matthew 5:14–16). Above all, remember to give love and accept love.

One evening just before the great star of stage and screen, Mary Martin, was to go on stage in "South Pacific" on Broadway, a note was handed to her. It was from Oscar Hammerstein, one of the authors of the show who, at that moment, was on his death bed. The short, vibrant note read: "Dear Mary, a bell is not a bell 'til you ring it, a song's not a song 'til you sing it, love in your heart was not put there to stay, love isn't love 'til you give it away." After Mary's performance that night, many people rushed back stage to congratulate her. They said, "Mary, you did something to us tonight, what was it?" Blinking back the tears, Mary Martin read them the note, then she said, "Tonight I gave my love away."

Love is active, it isn't passive. The gift of our Father's love to us was His only son, Jesus, who took our place on the cross, loving us that we might love, giving to us that we might give.

In this ministry, I have given and received. "You bring a smile to many troubled people's faces," read one inmate's letter. "You help them to see that everything isn't as bad as it seems and that God is there for them. I am a living witness . . . "

All of the gratitude I have received I offer to God, for He is the true source of their renewed spirit. "I just can't wait to be released. I have such a different outlook on life now that I have God and have wonderful people like you in my life." Another inmate wrote, "You have been my only special friend, and a second mother for me all through my ordeal. I felt bad that I could not do anything for you . . ."

It is not so much the good that we do, but the love that prompts our action and makes it efficacious. We all know, and sense, when we are totally loved by another. Even the infant in the crib can sense the mother, the father and even the nurse that emanates love.

Where do we get that love? Only God, the Holy Spirit, can bestow it upon us. Hence, the necessity of constant prayer and recourse to Him. Only by God's grace can we love the sinner, the prisoner, the ingrate — God's love flowing from us to those around us.

Pray for the gift of strength. The Holy Spirit gives us this gift of strength, to become fully alive in God's unending love, to live that same love and boldly acclaim it to others.

God has bestowed upon me a great love for young people, for those considered to be unloving and unlovable by society. This love is rooted in my love for Him. I pray that you too may be called by this great love for God.

An inmate has written:

> Day and night I cry. My heart breaks when I remember the past. Here in exile my heart is breaking . . . (Ps. 42)
>
> My friends and neighbors will not come near me; even my family keeps away from me . . . (Ps. 38)
>
> But you, dear Sister, are a true friend to one in need. Like a butterfly, very slight but definitely not fragile, you go about your daily God-appointed duties and bring the hope of the Lord's Word to me and my fellow inmates. We "will sing about what you and Our Lord have done." (Ps. 138)

"The Lord strengthens those who are weak and tired
. . . but those who trust in the Lord for help will find their
strength renewed. They will rise on wings . . . " (Isaiah 40)

"Happy are those whose greatest desire is to do what
God requires; God will satisfy them fully!" (Mt. 5:6)

Sister, may you be amply rewarded for your caring
heart, now and forever. Amen.

If all of us — inmates, citizens, government, churches and
ministers — work together with God and each other, the jails
and prisons of this country will shake with the transforming
power of Our Lord Jesus Christ . . . much as the earth shook that
Resurrection Morning nearly two thousand years ago.

I have been blessed in this ministry, and owe its rewards to
the many inmates. Together, we embarked on profound searches
for true spirituality. The inmates have been a source of inspiration, encouragement and joy. They have taught me to put greater
trust in God, reminded me of the necessity of faith in our lives
and demonstrated the power of human love in action.

It is God who asks us to use our eyes as His to see them, to
use our ears as His to hear them, to use our hands as His to
touch them, to use our mouth as His to spread His word, and to
use our feet as His to show them the way. And it is through God's
example that I have loved them and accepted their love in return.

Without the many contributions of the inmates, this book
would not be possible. All of their pain and hope, fears and
dreams, doubt and love lie within me forever.

After 14 years of ministering to inmates who have been processed through Chicago's Cook County Correctional Center, Sister Josephine no longer makes weekly visits to the jail. She has retired to the Missionary Sisters of the Sacred Heart's senior sisters' residence in Philadelphia, where she continues to correspond with the many inmates she has come to know so well.

To contact Sister Josephine, write her at:

6701 Callowhill Rd., Philadelphia, PA, 19151.

Index